T0128552

Reading

the

Unwritten

Teal L. Gray

authorHOUSE®

AuthorHouse™
1663 Liberty Drive
Bloomington, IN 47403
www.authorhouse.com
Phone: 1 (800) 839-8640

Published by AuthorHouse 01/15/2020

ISBN: 978-1-7283-4333-4 (sc)
ISBN: 978-1-7283-4334-1 (hc)
ISBN: 978-1-7283-4340-2 (e)

Print information available on the last page.

Any people depicted in stock imagery provided by Getty Images are models,
and such images are being used for illustrative purposes only.
Certain stock imagery © Getty Images.

Scripture quotations marked KJV are from the Holy Bible, King James Version
(Authorized Version). First published in 1611. Quoted from the KJV Classic
Reference Bible, Copyright © 1983 by The Zondervan Corporation.

Scripture quotations marked NASB are taken from the New American
Standard Bible®, Copyright © 1960, 1962, 1963, 1968, 1971, 1972, 1973,
1975, 1977, 1995 by The Lockman Foundation. Used by permission.

Scripture quotations marked NIV are taken from the Holy Bible, New
International Version®. NIV®. Copyright © 1973, 1978, 1984 by International
Bible Society. Used by permission of Zondervan. All rights reserved. [Biblica]

Scripture quotations marked NLT are taken from the Holy Bible, New Living
Translation, copyright © 1996, 2004, 2007. Used by permission of Tyndale House
Publishers, Inc. Carol Stream, Illinois 60188. All rights reserved. Website

Scripture quotations marked NKJV are taken from the New King James Version.
Copyright © 1982 by Thomas Nelson, Inc. Used by permission. All rights reserved.

The Holy Bible, Berean Study Bible, BSB
Copyright ©2016, 2018 by Bible Hub
Used by Permission. All Rights Reserved Worldwide.

This book is printed on acid-free paper.

CONTENTS

DEDICATION

To the most glorious gifts given to me in this lifetime, my daughters Melanie and Tiffany. You have every piece of my heart; you are my constant flames; my "True North."

ACKNOWLEDGMENTS

*A*ll thanks and glory to God who is the giver of all gifts. Blessings to all the Souls who have gone before me who's gentle breaths from Heaven blow clear my life's path, that I stumble less and help others more.

To everyone reading this book, I give you my support and faith in your abilities to create a life you have only dreamed of, degree by degree.

FOREWORD

My life is filled with entities and spirits most cannot see. I do not see them all the time but often feel them near. I spent years trying to keep them away, but they were there whether I decided to acknowledge them or not. Realizing this, I put my fears aside and turned my battle into a dance with this unseen but very real world. It can be a scary experience. Anyone telling you they have never been afraid, or do not have at least a healthy respect of the unseen world hasn't fully experienced it.

This book lets you in on some of my experiences and about me discovering and using my intuition, Tea Leaf and other divination methods to help others and myself to predict the future.

But really? It's about a journey we take together as reader and storyteller to uncover ancient truths, unused talents and evolve our souls to a higher level of abilities and understanding that can help us find our true path in this life.

It's designed for people who like me, are naturally curious and want to "know" everything! But also, people who struggle with the question is this against the laws of God? Is it unwise to dabble in the unknown and paranormal world? Will this harm me or my family in any way like depicted in movies and television?

From all of my studies and experiences I believe your gifts are from God, The Source, A Higher Power and you have nothing to fear or hide.

A whole new world of abilities and possibilities are possible to bring into your life.

Teal Gray

INTRODUCTION

The trajectory is a path, progression, or line of development; a mapped-out intention of where you are going in your life. Do you have one? Or does your life seem to be out of control most of the time?

When piloting a vessel, the result depends entirely on degrees.

Shining a light down a taught string only reveals the end point of a current direction.

The current angle you see is different depending on the pilot's current trajectory if they make a different decision that will change directions and the path altered.

That same taught string in one direction can be just one of many, creating a web of possibilities, places and people good and bad, that can tangle you up and hold you down like the sticky web of a spider or help break you free from what's holding you back from your best course.

Our life's scenarios we create. By the movement of the degrees of our decisions; you are the pilot!

True north is not magnetic north. Land based true north stays constant while magnetic north is flexible. Why? Our Earth has an iron core. A vertical pole connects the North and South Poles. As the earth moves within its outer part there is a magnetic field that is generated. If you are seeking guidance from a compass, it will point to the magnetic North Pole.

True north on a map is shown using latitude and longitudinal lines. The north celestial pole shows us the direction of astronomical true north in the sky. If you look at maps published by US Geological Survey, you will see true north marked by a line ending in a five-point star.

Most people never get still long enough to clearly examine their life and where they are on its web. Many fearing what they might discover. It's not easy going through a session of self-examination. Remember, looking at it from the perspective of an afterlife review will be much harder.

Are the people currently in your life a calm, steady guide like the true north we so desperately need to reach our full potential? If not, they can create a drama filled reactionary life rather than an intentionally engaging one.

Find out who you truly are and what you want. I always tell my clients that time is our most precious commodity. We unfortunately do not know how much we came into this world with or how much we have left.

What means the most to you? Family, friends, your job, money? Get honest with yourself about what you value and what you are willing to trade time for. They are the bits of your life you spend each day. Every decision we make every day, all day long, until we run out of it. Don't waste a second of it on guilt, fear and trying to change people and situations. It will never be worth the price in the end.

As I look at my life, now clearly past the storms and showers of spring and the growth it brings. Summer loves, and warm thoughts make me smile, with part of me there. My hand now feels the tall wheat harvest of life's autumn. Full of memories and gratitude, not yet feeling the chill of life's winter.

I have that perspective we have been talking about in my life, my trajectory. It guides me, and I hope this book will guide you in a way that from this point forward you will have the tools to make your life not just a journey, but one with a true north as well.

Many blessings,
Teal L. Gray Rev., N.D.

1

UNSEEN CONNECTIONS

*U*nseen realms can be a controversial subject. Passionate voices at elevated levels can be heard discussing the reality of an unseen, yet real world interacting with ours.

One side will only believe empirical evidence. To this group, if it cannot be proven using scientific methods then it should be dismissed as an odd occurrence at best. Meanwhile, someone who believes they had a personal interaction with an angel, spirit, or entity of some kind will not back down when relaying their truth of a usually profound and sometimes life changing experience.

I will not try to make you choose a side. Rather, my hope is by bringing you thoughts on religion, sacred sites, and many years of study, you will draw your own conclusions as to what you believe, and what is merely an entertaining idea or story.

There is no wrong answer. We are all on a journey. Our bodies do not animate our life force. Our life force animates our bodies, moving us along this learning experience called life. This beautiful and complicated world we live in is much like the inner workings of our bodies, and in a third connection, the ethereal or unseen realm.

Both the earth, and our bodies, are made up of about seventy percent water. Water can be changed, but it is never gone. Ice can be melted, by heating it to become a liquid. Heat it further, and the resulting steam seems to disappear.

Think of your physical body as the ice, giving the appearance of being solid. The physical components that are part of your body, are fluid in the sense of being a living, ever changing system which I will compare as liquid for my example.

Think of your physical body as the ice, which was solid and considered physically here. The physical components that are part of your body, are fluid in the sense of being a living, ever changing system, like the liquid that could be seen and touched. Many will still be hanging in there with me when I say, the ice (your body), and the liquid (everything that makes up your internal and external physical self) was real. Now, all that reality of form merely changed once more. Not making it any less real when it became steam, or when your life force, (soul) leaves your body when you die. The difference now, is that it disappeared, and we cannot see it. However, vapor or steam is very real. At the right temperature, it can power a train! which in my mind that is real!

If you are now scratching your head, you can reverse the steps to give you back something you can hold in your hands and call real. How? Well, if you decided to capture the steam, then take the container you captured it in, observe the steam will turn once again into water. Take the container of water, put it in the freezer, and you are right back where we started with solid, "real" ice. I think it is also a way to think of the possibility of reincarnation.

Reincarnation is the belief that after death, we begin a new life, in a new body. The Latin meaning of the word "reincarnation," means, "entering the flesh again," Like my example using ice as a representation of the physical body, we took it through the steps to becoming ice once again. It was reincarnated from steam, to a solid state once more.

I believe the same gravitational pull between the Earth and the Moon affecting the ocean tides, also affects the water in our bodies, and possibly in different dimensions, in varying degrees.

Many paranormal investigators report heightened activity being captured on a full moon, the best being the classic, stormy, full moon night. Why? Because the spirits use the additional electrical charges in the air, to manifest themselves or move things. Spaces are generally quieter in the deep of night, so we notice activity, and faint sounds we might miss otherwise, are easier to hear.

All, but a small part of the body is made up of oxygen, carbon, hydrogen, nitrogen, calcium and phosphorus. What does that mean? About ninety percent of the human body's mass, is made of the elements of stardust. Nearly the same as the earth. Look up into the night sky, and think about the fact that you, and the earth you are standing on, are made up of what once was once the inside of an exploded star. You have heard the saying, "It is in our DNA." Well, the earth we walk on, the bodies we live in, are all part of the stars in the heavens above! We are connected.

Saturn, Mars, Jupiter and Mercury, do not produce their own light. Yet we see them, because of reflected sunlight. At least some people would agree the planets I listed are real. But if the sunlight reflecting, did not allow us to see them, and they became suddenly invisible to us, would they no longer be real because of the change in our perception of them?

We are not static, solid bodies. We, like the planets and the stars, are always changing. The earth changes and adapts to natural and manmade disasters. Look at your skin. In about a month, it will not be the same skin you see today, it will have regenerated itself. Part of what once made your body's covering, is gone. But the essence of you is still here no matter how much of your skin or organs regenerate.

What does all of this have to do with the spirit or unseen realm?

Like us, like the earth, like the stars, and every other living thing, change as part of the natural process. The examples I gave, hopefully help you see how we are made to adapt, to change, and no matter what form, still exist. To be considered real, and interactive in some way, even if different than when we were in a solid form. But just because something is in a different form when you originally knew it, does not make it any less real. Seen or unseen, we are all connected to part of a larger collective whole.

Electricity as another example, cannot be created or destroyed, it can only change from one form to another. When we are alive, we have electrical energy, a current, running through our bodies. What happens to that electricity when we die?

It does not stay with the dead body. It leaves unseen into the atmosphere, and places unknown. Every paranormal investigator I know, has a device to pick up electromagnetic fields believed to be emitted by ghosts. Perhaps this is the form of a trace amount of energy still connected to us, when we leave the solid mass of our body. Maybe it stays with us when we transition into a spirit, or unseen form? If so, why would that be any less real? It is after all, just a different form of us.

Literally billions of people around the world center their lives on an unprovable, unseen, spiritual realm. Following some form of ritual, prayer, or meditation to various practices or gods; believing, and reporting on miracles happening in their lives, seeing loved ones who have crossed over, and being saved, or warned of danger by angels. Throughout time we have fought wars because of our beliefs. We feel the need to validate our relationships with the blessing of whatever God, or gods we worship. We baptize or christen our children and ourselves because we believe an unprovable, unseen spiritual force will protect us even after death. Why then is it so difficult to believe that we go on living in some form after death? Why so impossible to accept angels, spirits and demons are surrounding us here on earth?

Is it likely that so many people around the world would report paranormal encounters if at least a some of them were not real?

It is hard to dismiss. Not every person around the world can be delusional. It is statistically improbable. Would the stories and belief in the unseen continue throughout time, generation after generation? Not likely. They would be dismissed, and new practices surrounding a revised belief system would take over.

PREPARATION AND
INTUITION

*M*any people clear their homes, workspaces and cars on a regular basis to push out negative energy and make space for positive higher vibrating energy to flow in and assist for our highest and greatest good.

It will make such a difference. I have also created a spray formula that not only has sage, but I include holy water, salts, and sacred oils from my sacred site travels along with home grown herbs. This is a very powerful blend and it is loved by many people all over the world. If you wish to purchase my spray or any of my other infused products go to thelavendercrow.com, You can never have too many blessings, right?

To burn a smudge stick, place it in an abalone shell or some other heat-proof container partially filled with sand or salt to hold the smudge upright. Light the tip, blow it out and direct the smoke around your body and/or the space you wish to "clear". You may also set the wand in a container and use a feather or your hand to direct the smoke where needed. To extinguish, invert smudge into the sand or salt to smother until it is extinguished and save the remainder of the bundle for another time. A sage bundle, or stick as many call it, can be used many times if cared for properly. Some situations call for so much clearing that it is possible to use up the entire stick depending on the length made or purchased.

Use any type of **Sage** to smudge to purify the mind, body and spirit before praying, purifying the atmosphere & dispersing negativity. It is also used to purify sacred items such as ceremonial clothing, paranormal investigating equipment and feathers. I even use it on my vehicles! I also make my own potpourri mix and set it out in bowls, toss handfuls into outdoor fires or indoor fireplaces. I put little bags of it in my vehicles to continually bless them and it also smells wonderful.

Another favorite clearing item I use is **Palo Santo** meaning "holy wood." This aromatic incense was used by the Incas and people of the Andes for centuries. It comes from a mystical tree that has a heavenly smell and calming effect. I believe it also enhances creativity and clears negative low-level energy from your space.

Yerba Santa is a holy herb also used to protect your environment. I use it to promote the energy of love, empowerment and beauty. It helps greatly in the release of emotional pain stored in the heart chakra.

As with candles or anything you light and burn, please take care and never leave unattended. Also, be careful not to burn yourself when extinguishing your purifying tool of choice.

Crystals really work quickly to block negative energy, especially if you are an empath and sensitive to picking up on other people's thoughts and energy. Black stones are my favorite, especially black tourmaline and shungite. Amber is also particularly good for protection. I make sure to purify my crystals and stones regularly. I like to wash mine in captured rainwater and set them in the sun to recharge. You can also do this by the moonlight if you prefer. Always go with the method that feels right for you. And that often means creating your own system of cleansing and recharging them.

Visualization takes a little more work. You will need to find a quiet time where you are alone in calm surroundings to meditate and visualize. Simply take some deep breathes then close your eyes and imagine you are surrounded by a safe barrier through which no harmful energy can get through. If you are being bothered by neighbors, you can imagine a safe shield of energy surrounding your home, or even your car. If you wish to send the negative energy back to the sender, then visualize a mirror around you so that the bad vibes bounce right off back to the sender.

Mirrors of any size work very effectively. I have them everywhere in my homes, property, and workspaces. You can put a small mirror in a front window of your home that wards away bad energy from entering or wear mirrored, reflective or silver jewelry. It will deflect negative energy. Remember when you put it on to wear it with intent of your desired outcome and work you want it to do for you.

Everyone Is Intuitive

The more you acknowledge it, the stronger and more accurate it gets. Intuition is a natural ability that makes it possible to know something without any proof. It's just a feeling that guides us without us fully understanding why.

I like to use the example of playing a musical instrument. Some people can play by ear. Without lessons, they just pick up an instrument and quickly play a tune they have heard or can make up a melody from what's playing in their head. Others need lessons. Sometimes many lessons to play even a simple tune. Both types can play an instrument. They are gifted with that ability, but one of them accesses that gift on a naturally higher level that the other type. One is not better than the other. Not more important. Just gifted differently. So, don't think because you aren't running around telling everyone's fortune that you got skipped when God was handing out gifts and talents. You have them. We just need to enhance what you already have into something that is a useful tool in your life.

Intuition often shows up as a fleeting thought we probably dismiss as coincidence or imagination. For example, the telephone rings and you intuitively know who it is before answering. I believe that everything happens for a reason. From my childhood, I was taught to pay attention to signs and symbols as messages being given to us. There have been many times I was running late and no matter what, I just couldn't seem to get out the door. Then when I finally am on the road, I find out I avoided a terrible wreck that I may have been in if I left when I originally wanted to.

How does Intuitive information come to you? The most common is physically. That gut reaction to a person or a situation. All living creatures possess intuition or instinct. This is hardwired into our DNA. Fight or flight. Everything vibrates from the nucleus of an atom to the molecules of our blood, our brain, sound, plants, animals, all the way into outer space. We are connected to the intertwined intelligence of the universe. Every living creature is connected to the universe and us as well. Telepathic Communication between humans and animals is very common and possible. Did you know it is proven that Dolphins and Bats can hear the sound Created by the stars? A star's surface is constantly on the move. Its surface has moving plasma which accumulates different elements drawn by the pull of gravity which produces a sound, or a melody.

When people describe tragic events, they have lived through such as earthquakes, forest fires, and tornadoes, many say their first sign something was wrong was that the animals were all going away from the danger.

Secondly, through our emotions. We know instantly when something doesn't feel right.

Thirdly, mental communication. That voice in our head telling us what to do. Or what not to do.

The fourth way we receive intuitive insights is Spiritually. We may in prayer or meditation, be given what many call divine messages from a higher power.

Pay attention, keep a journal to log the times you felt you were receiving intuitive assistance. This will help you trust the information you get when you get it because you can look back and see when it was correct. Never think you can skip this step. You will not remember even seemingly amazing instances as time passes. Or details that could prove important may fade as time passes.

TOOLS AND TRAPS

 $\mathcal{W}$ hen dealing with the paranormal, unseen realm, I urge caution. You must use the same care and protection whether you are using Tarot Cards, Tea leaves, Spirit Boxes or Ouija Boards. These things and many others are tools for connecting with unseen spirits. You can never truly be certain with whom you are speaking. You can only be as careful as possible.

Throughout history we curious humans have sought to find out what lies ahead in our future, or in the great beyond after we die.

Many times, it starts out as harmless fun, something you don't believe is real. Then things can quickly get out of hand if you don't know how to properly use the tools at your disposal. It would be my advice to stay away from all of it if possible. But since I know you won't, here are some cautionary tales to help guide you in your decisions.

Heart of the House

Can the actions of disturbing the dead, and calling them forth, last for decades? I've asked that question for many years, with one night in mind when the wind was raging like it was coming from all directions at once. I still remember the sounds the house made that night. It was more than a howling wind. It was much, much more. The events of that night still affect the house to this day.

The pretty red brick home sat proudly on a one-acre corner lot in Dallas, Texas. I was just three years old in 1964, when we moved in. Long before there were shopping centers surrounding it, there was a picture book farm across the street. I spent lots of time on the front porch looking across what was at the time only two lanes of very little traffic, onto beautiful pastures with horses plowing fields and cows grazing. Every corner of our property was filled with fruit trees, and flowering bushes, and the largest sweetest smelling wisteria bush covering the carport that I have ever seen, even to this day.

My tenth birthday had just passed in mid-October 1971. Finally, having made it into the double-digit years, I thought that made me old enough to hang out with my older brothers and their friends. They always said no when I asked before, except that night, they looked at each other when I asked to be at the party, laughed and said, "Sure, tonight it just might be fun."

My parents had left earlier in the day for a Halloween party at my Aunt's house and would not be back until the following afternoon. They had no concerns about leaving me with three adult brothers, but the darker the night grew, and the stranger the people arriving at our house got, I did.

It was the first Halloween I didn't have a costume. I suppose I thought it would make me seem childish. All the other girls arriving were in sleek long black dresses, and carrying bundles of candles and sticks, some with gypsy looking bandannas and ribbons tied in their hair. I remember thinking how odd it was that most of the girls were barefooted, it was October. Granted, Texas was warmer than most states this time of year, but it was still cold.

All the guys were wearing black, except for this one friend of my middle brother that was appropriately, in my mind, nicknamed "Loser." He was all in white, I mean even his shoes and jacket, everything. Wait, did I say jacket? I would later realize what was thrown over his arm was a full-length white cape.

The party started. The music was blaring, and you could hardly understand what people were saying. They were all laughing and drinking, excitedly talking about whatever was happening later. The girls were going room to room, drawing all the curtains and replacing the comforting lamplight, with the spookier flicker of candlelight, from what must have been a hundred black candles throughout the house. I had never seen black candles before. My mom only used white ones on the dining room table, maybe red at Christmas, but never black.

The party had been going on for hours, and I stayed out of the way most of the time, just in case my brothers changed their minds, and sent me to stay with our elderly neighbors, the Gibson's.

While dodging flailing arms, and spinning bodies dancing through our house, I ended up in a little side room we had that was like a small study or den. There were only a handful of people talking quietly, and there sitting on my favorite couch was my brother Jessie's best friend David! He was playing some sort of card game intently on the coffee table, and a girl was writing down what he told her. I never saw this game before, and I was curious.

"Sit down here by me." David said patting the couch. "I'm going to teach you how to blow someone's mind." I sat down nervously. Partly because I was, but mostly because I had a secret crush on David. He was always so cool, drove a big blue motorcycle, and had the brightest blue eyes to match.

These cards looked funny to me. "These look weird." I said.

He quickly spun to face me and very seriously said, "Never ever say anything bad about them. They don't like it, and you don't want to piss them off understand?"

"Sure, sorry, I", but before I could finish stumbling the words from my mouth, he put the deck of cards in my hands and covered them with his. I'm not going to lie and tell you I remember what he said at that point, but I still remember the loud pounding of my heart in my ears at a moment we were having, whatever it was.

He told me the story of each card as he laid them out, and they were so colorful and beautifully drawn. I was fascinated. He said I was about to do my first reading. I didn't know what that meant and didn't care. I was knee to knee with my crush, and he was talking to me. So, I followed his instructions as the girl with the note pad sat herself down cross legged on the floor in front of us. I shuffled and dropped cards and apologized to everyone and the cards repeatedly, because I wasn't sure what would happen if they got pissed off, and I didn't want to find out. I remember getting drawn into the cards.

My focus left David completely and shifted to the cards that seemed to "tell" me where to place them. Only in the background and beyond my caring, would I occasionally hear a, "That's right, good, you're a natural." from David.

The girl took notes, and I noticed her at times, consider David's eyes and smile at something the cards said by their position on the table. This went on for a long time, until a call went out through the house, "It's time!'

Faster than you can imagine possible, everyone from throughout the house, front and back yards went running to the big room my brothers shared when they were younger. No one used it anymore, and it was completely empty. My parents couldn't decide what to do with it. Tonight, I guess it was decided for them.

It had been transformed, into a sort of candlelit forest, with a big circle drawn on the old wooden floor, in the center of the room, with a star inside. There was a table at one end with a black tablecloth on it and stuff I had never seen before. Knives and big goblet looking things and more sticks, colorful rocks, plants and a Ouija board. They had all been playing with the board and I missed it learning about cards from David.

Maybe I will find out what it's all about later. The music was turned off, but my ears were still ringing as several girls carried incense around the room, making it smoky and hard to breathe in. Bodies were packed in side by side, all in black.

Then, in walks Loser, all in white. His bright blonde hair and cold grey eyes barely seen beneath the hood of the full cascading white cape. I never liked him, but he looked strangely gorgeous in that moment. I had never seen anything like it, this, gathering.

There were two other guys with Loser that I had never seen at our house before. I didn't like the look of them and could see how they would be friends. One of them handed him a big book wrapped in a black towel or something. It looked old but I didn't dare go closer to see because, he never liked me either.

Loser held up the book and everyone went silent. He started talking about this gathering, and the importance of the ceremony being done at what was now 3:00 a.m., and in the heart of the house. He starting saying things from the book I could not understand and as the crowd got more intense, I slipped out of the room and watched from the other end of the hallway, alone in the dark.

Loser was yelling now, switching between English and something I couldn't understand. He said, "Focus on this space, this heart of the house. Tonight, it brings lives through it, as we give life to it!"

I couldn't see what was happening, everyone in the room was surrounding him, but I did not like being there, and was just about to slip outside when a voice from behind me said, "Don't be scared, it's Halloween fun, it's not real." I thought I might have to borrow the heart of the house, because mine just stopped. I was so scared in that moment, I felt like my blood drained from me. I jolted around to see my brother Bruce. I jumped into his arms as if I was half my age. Told him this felt bad, and we should get away from it.

He explained that as you get older, you must make Halloween parties scary to be any fun. It was just a show, none of it was real, and everyone knew that. He offered to take me next door, but I wanted to see what would happen next. I was relieved that it was just pretend, and some of the people were in on it, and just acting, it was all a joke.

Suddenly, the wind began raging outside, like it was coming from all directions at the same time. Branches were striking the windows in the room where they were all chanting now. The house did seem to breathe, although I'm sure it was just because of the wind, and it was an older home. People were yelling out, and the two bad friends of Loser, start throwing some sort of liquid onto people and they were rubbing on themselves. What was it? As people moved around, the candlelight illuminated the wet liquid on their arms, legs and faces. It shimmered in the flashes of light as a dark red color. Was that blood? There was talk about cemetery dirt, and go get the tombstone, when a fight broke out. My brothers were fighting with Loser and his friends! They threw them out of the house. I ran out the back door and hid just outside watching as the fight grew.

With the bad people finally gone, my brothers and their dozen or so friends that were still there, cleaned everything up like it never happened. My brothers were edgy and shaken. When everyone was gone, they kept checking the window locks, and door locks. They decided to take turns sleeping and keeping watch. We were all to stay together in the living room on couches. Apparently, there might be retaliation for ending the ceremony and fighting with Loser.

I had so many questions, but I heard and saw enough to know to just be quiet and lay low.

I settled into the love seat, and as I was drifting off to sleep, I heard music, but very faint. I thought maybe it was a car radio outside, and Loser was back to cause more trouble. I whispered to my brother who had already heard it. He woke the other two, and we followed the sound. It was coming from what I now call the ceremony room. But that room was empty again? Once inside, all we heard was the creaking floorboards under our feet. No music. All the sudden, the radio on top of the refrigerator in the kitchen on the other side of the house came on full blast! We all screamed and ran to the kitchen. Somebody must have broken in!

My brother Scott quickly switched it off. The others checked the house again. Nobody was inside but us. We went back to the living room and sat in silence. Each trying to make sense out of what just happened. Again, kitchen radio turns itself on full blast. We all run in; Scott jerks the plug out of the wall. Another search of the house, closets, under beds, everywhere, but nobody is in there but us! My brother Scott tells me not to worry about it, daylight is coming, and the radio was probably on a timer that kicked on and got stuck. Yeah, I like that idea, I can live with that.

The fatigue that comes from fear must have won out, because we all woke up at the same time with a knocking at the door. It was morning, and David was back bearing donuts to talk about the crazy stuff that went down the night before. Apparently, Loser was into Black Magic, David explained. He himself, was only into the good stuff, the light stuff.

My brothers said they went along with Loser's party idea because they thought it was just a joke to ramp up the vibe of Halloween night. When they realized, he was not kidding, and it was real, they threw him out. They told David they felt silly now, but the heat of the moment kept them on edge all night, jumping out of their skin when the radio turned on, twice. David laughed with them and they turned the conversation to girls, and that was my queue to leave.

Several weeks passed, and unfortunately in the remodeling of the house, I was assigned to sleep permanently in, you guessed it, the ceremony room. My parents never knew what went on that Halloween night, so in their mind they were giving me the biggest bedroom in the house.

Even after I had been in there and cleaned it repeatedly, I would still find a splatter of blood along a crack between a floorboard and the wall, or a speck of it on the dark wooden sliding closet doors.

I never knew everything what went on in that room the night it became the ceremony room. There were many hours I was occupied learning to read Tarot cards and just plain staying out of the way.

The house felt different, we explained away, hearing voices calling our name, or unexplained noises, we all knew something was different, darker.

The house, no matter what you changed about it, no longer felt safe or happy. It moved from a feeling, to more outrageous happenings. Heavy wooden closet doors in my room would slide open on their own if front of even a group of people in broad daylight. Then my brothers started seeing a shadowy tall man walking from my room only to disappear midway down the hall.

Was this connected to what I suspect was a stolen headstone by Loser? Shadows would appear at night on the drapes as if someone walking behind you, yet no one was there. We would all be perfectly happy on a family outing, only to start bickering and fighting over nothing as soon as we were home.

The years passed, and the heavy presence never left. I wondered, even though the ceremony was cut short, had it gone on long enough to open a portal of some kind? Had the Ouija board brought spirits in? How else could the instant change and weird experiences that none of us ever had before be explained away?

I was asleep in my room one afternoon; my brother was visiting with our mother in the living room. I was starting to wake to the feeling of someone softly brushing my long hair back from my face. Stroking my face with the back of their hand ever so gently. I smiled, opening my eyes expecting it to be my mother, only to see a very pale and very dead woman sitting beside me, reaching for me once again.

I screamed and ran from my room without thinking where I was going. In a blind panic, I ran and probably would have died or been seriously injured, if my brother had not grabbed me just at the last moment before I went through the two-story plate glass windows. One of my biggest fears to this day, is the thought of waking up to see someone opposite me in bed that should not be there!

We finally moved out in 1980, after living there almost sixteen years. It was almost unrecognizable, by the time we left, from its once beautiful, peaceful original self. Driving by it sometimes I would see another for sale sign in the yard. Nobody stayed there very long.

I wondered what ultimately became of the house. Were the spirits still there?

Just this year 2016, I was searching for someone to read my cards. Although I was well able to read them myself, I wanted a second opinion on a couple of things. I searched for psychics in Dallas and to my disbelief, my old address popped up on the computer screen before me! I called the number, got no answer, left a message telling them I was so surprised to see my old house was now a psychic reader's business. I also asked, "Are they all still there? The spirits I mean?"

I waited two weeks, still no reply. I called again and left a new message with my number but this time, I gave no name, and did not ask about the spirits. I got a call back right away! I tried to set an appointment but was told stopping by was best. People are no shows for appointments usually, and she preferred walk in clients. I agreed to come in soon, but right before I hung up, I couldn't help myself, I had to ask again.

"Are they all still there, the spirits?"

After a long silence, she said, "Oh, it's you. Yes, there are many of them, they mostly stay in one room, nobody goes in there. I keep the door bolted shut."

I said, "Is it the big corner room with all the windows and big wooden closet doors with deep claw marks on the inside of the doors, and blood stains you can't get rid of?" I rattled off, trying to get all my burning questions answered before she hung up.

"Yes," she curtly. Before I could reply, the woman abruptly hung up, leaving me with only the deadline dial tone to answer the rest of my questions.

We Need You to Unlock this Board

Other than a Ouija board that had been brought into our house for a Halloween party when I was ten, I never even saw a board before, or had any experience or teaching about them. I had been instructed by my German grandmother from the time I was five in reading tea leaves, and started reading Tarot cards when I was ten, but boards, never, until I was sixteen.

My mother had become close with my eldest brother Scott's girlfriend Terri. Terri had interesting friends I would come to realize, but not before I unknowingly opened a portal that I had no idea how to close.

I have always been a collector of antiques and loved the history and stories each piece holds. So, it was not difficult to get me to join my mother and Terri for some ladies get together in a big historic Dallas mansion promised to be filled to the rafters with beautiful antiques.

I was so excited pulling up the long driveway to a mansion like those you see in the movies. I was greeted quickly and with lots of excitement by the group of ladies pouring out of the house to scoop me from the car to what was waiting for me.

They took turns grabbing my hand and touching my hair as if I was a new doll they had just collected. I was not used to so much fanfare and I liked it even though I couldn't imagine why I was so prized at this gathering. Everyone was much older than me. The owner of the home was in her nineties, joined by her daughter in her seventies and my mother, Terri and four others, a mix of thirties to fifties.

I commented on the beauty of the home and the antiques and expressed my thanks for being invited to their gathering. The owner moved forward quickly I felt for her age and took my hands into hers and staring into my eyes said, "My dear, you speak of these antiques as a rare find. To me you are a rare find. I want to introduce you to an old friend a little later."

I replied with a thank you, but all that came to mind was where was this old friend. She was in her nineties, so maybe they were resting. We were ushered past the grand dining room I had hoped we would dine in, into a farther back room of the house off the kitchen and den area.

They seated me at a very old table that I estimated was from the late 1700's. It was beautiful and had carvings I had never seen before along the underside, and on several spots before the ornate claw feet resting solidly on the floor. For a small table, it was heavy. The others were seated on couches, chairs and several other tables all facing me. There was an empty chair opposite me, and I asked if anyone would like to join my table. No one answered. I was brought a lovely Sunday roast plate of food on antique china. I was given a beautiful cut glass and gold goblet of a rich odd tasting red liquid, that to this day I hope was punch. The old silver knife and fork were heavy in my nervous hands, but I loved the experience of being there up to this point.

The glances from woman to woman became more frequent, and I could feel the anxiety level in the room grow, as they waited for me to finish the plate of food, they had given me. I was still hungry but was so uncomfortable being watched by all of them, I politely put my napkin over my plate to their relief, and it was quickly taken away.

I started to feel a little like the Thanksgiving turkey that loves all the food and attention but can't shake the feeling something bad is about to happen. And it was.

The once statue like group of ladies came quickly to life. Closing curtains, lighting candles and getting themselves situated in front of me as if a show was about to begin. It was the seventies, and after growing up in the sixties I never knew what weirdness the grownups were into.

I was quiet and very shy at the time, so I just sat there.

From a dark little closet, off to the side of the room the owner, brought a dark piece of wood toward me. I couldn't see what it was until she placed it before me on the table. She said, "We need you to unlock this board."

My mouth fell open, startled by her piercing gray eyes, I told her I had no idea what she was talking about. She stood up very straight and said, "Girl you have been brought here by your family with the promise you had the gifts needed to open this board!" I glanced around her body to ask my mother and Terri what was going on.

They said, "We know you can talk to spirits." I felt like I had been dropped into the middle of a television show with no idea of the storyline or where this plot was going. It was just a surreal feeling. I looked back to the agitated woman before me and said again that I have no knowledge of whatever this board was, and that I had never touched one.

She went on to say it was passed down to her from her relatives from the Salem Witch trial days. For many generations, it had sat idle but, she explained, before she died, she wanted to see it work, just once.

I just stared at the board for a moment. So many emotions were running through me, but mostly fear. This board before me felt alive, even though they said it hadn't worked in generations. I lost my focus on self and the group before me. The board was calling to me somehow, instructing me in a gentle leading way.

I listened, and we began to converse, not in spoken words, but in my mind. It led me to pick up the heavy crystal looking piece laying on top of it. I took it into my hands and it quickly became warm. I looked up and the owner of the house was no longer standing there.

A thin blonde woman was there. She said with a nervous smile, "I see you can do this." And with that she sat at the opposite end of the table from me.

In a quiet voice, she said, this is a very old board. I would like to help you speak to the spirits that come forward through the board. Through the board? I had never thought of where the spirits came from, I just knew they were always around.

She explained we were to ever so lightly touch our fingertips to each side of the planchette. I glanced at her as she touched the crystal object, then so did I.

Things moved very quickly at this point, there was no learning curve or time to process what was happening. To my shock, the crystal piece began to move vigorously around the wooden board to symbols and letters so quickly I couldn't make sense of it.

The group of ladies were gasping, and the owner was clapping and from the corner of my vision I could see her jumping up and down. Several of the women were scribbling on notebooks and asking questions of the blonde woman working the board with me. My head was spinning trying to understand what was happening. How could this be real, and who was moving the piece around? It wasn't me pushing it in fact the blonde girl and myself lost touch of it several times, yet it still moved!

I heard loud noises coming from upstairs. It sounded like furniture was banging around and there were heavy footsteps. With this the owner grew concerned. She said she had a little boy spirit who lived upstairs, and she didn't want him harmed.

She started rattling off demands of me to give the board. With that, I swear to you the table I was seated at, that the board was on, started to lift on different corners almost like it was dancing. Then it got violent. I stood up and moved away. Everything stopped, the table landed with a bang on the wooden floor. The women were moving around scared and yelling, but I couldn't hear exactly what they were saying. I was so scared, and I had never seen or experienced anything like this in my life. Everything seemed to be in pause mode.

Then in one of the most chilling moments I can remember, the crystal slid toward me. I looked at the women all lined up in front of me like deer in the headlights, and at that moment I think they were afraid of me. The shy, quiet girl they lied to, and manipulated was controlling this board, this chaos. But was I? No, it was controlling me.

I liked that feeling of power, it overrode the fear, and my commonsense. I can't tell you why, but when I should have run, I sat back down and picked up the crystal.

The women all took turns inspecting the table and moved around it and held their hands on my knees, and those of my blonde accomplice.

I placed the crystal on the board. The women asked questions for me to then ask the board because it would not answer them.

They wanted to know why it would speak to me and not them. It answered, 'We used to kill together." What! I had never killed anyone. Of course, now I realize it must have been in a past life or lives.

All the women wanted to know then if the board liked them too. The answer was always no, even the blonde girl helping me did not escape the, "No!'

Throughout this time, I was being shown in my mind, ceremonies, fighting, and deaths dealt out without regard to sex or age in this vision. Oddly this did not affect me. It was just a matter of fact feeling, a memory I had forgotten, but felt no judgement over.

I was feeling so tired and I don't know how long this went on. Then the table started to dance again even with everyone trying to hold it down. At the same time the noises of furniture being knocked over upstairs started again and the sound of running feet.

The owner screamed, "They are hurting the boy I know it! Get her out of here, get her out!" Terri grabbed me by the arm and my mother was already out the door.

I looked back and remember the frightened face of the blonde lady, the running around, the beautiful old board still open and calling for me to come chat, but I am pulled away, with my arm still reaching back for it.

I never went back. I wasn't welcome. The house became a terrifying place of dark energy. The owner took very ill and died not long after that night I was told. I did not know how I brought the board to life; I also did not know how to close it. So, the spirits continued to use it as a passageway to our realm.

4

TEA LEAVES, WAX CASTING AND MORE

"Leaves are like pages in your life story."
Teal Gray

Tasseography, or more commonly called Tea Leaf Reading, interprets patterns and symbols as well as the placement of the tea leaves left in the cup. During the Victorian era it was a popular parlor game.

This is a straightforward way of doing a reading at home. If you want to use several age-old aids to your reading, put your wedding, or engagement ring on the back surface of the cup, or a picture of the person in question.

Is your question related to money or finances? Put a coin on the back surface of the cup.

If a big chunk of the leaves fall down on the saucer then it is taken as the first positive sign of your reading. Trouble and worries are leaving you.

If the fallen leaves form a pile, then money will soon be on the way to you.

If cup and saucer cannot be separated easily and the reader can lift the cup-saucer set as one unit, it is called a "Prophet's cup". You don't need to proceed. All your wishes will come true.

How to do your own tea leaf reading

You can read coffee grounds just as easily.

The truth is, you could throw dirt, molten iron, confetti, or anything that can form an image down and I will read it for you!

During this process please use your non dominant hand to hold the cup.

By that I mean if you are right-handed, hold the cup with your left hand. If left-handed, hold it with your right hand. If you happen to be ambidextrous, I suggest holding the cup cradled in both hands.

Wrap your dominant hand around the side of the cup, and if you feel inclined to do so, put your pointer finger into the tea for an extra connection.

Step 1: Chose your cup and your tea

Use a wide mouth or traditional style teacup. A mug will not work well because the tea leaves have a tendency to stay in the bottom or lower parts of the mug.

Almost any leaf tea will work. My personal preference is a blend of Earl Grey with herbal chamomile. If you do not mind the tiny floating bits, you can open a tea bag and sprinkle the tea into a cup of very warm water.

Step 2: Steep your tea and focus on your question

Green and black teas are usually ready in a minute or two, herbal teas take longer. I like to wait 3-5 minutes no matter what, just to focus the mind on the question at hand.

Step 3: Sip your tea and focus on your question.

Once your tea is cool enough, begin sipping it while focusing on your question. Focus on even breathing and try to bring your mind back to your question when it wanders. Some leaves will be floating in the cup and some sink faster. Leave a small amount of tea at the bottom of your cup.

Step 4: Swirl the last bit of tea in the cup counterclockwise three times and flip your cup over.

Hold your nearly empty teacup in your hand and give it three good swirls in a counterclockwise manner. The tea leaves will disperse around the interior of cup. Gently dump out the remaining liquid by turning your teacup over into a saucer.

Wait a few seconds before turning your cup back over. You want to give the tea a chance to drain out. Some drops of liquid will remain. You are now ready to read your tea leaves!

Step 5: Identifying the symbols, letters and numbers.

Pattern and symbol recognition will take practice so be patient with yourself, this is a skill to be learned over time. I first started to learn from my German Grandmother when I was five. I am in my fifties now and still learning! I used to watch her as she had her morning tea. I commented one day that she starred for so long into her empty cup, why didn't she just get some more to drink? She laughed and said I was way too young for these sorts of things but come sit close beside her and she would teach me what had been passed down for many generations. I definitely was too young for all the lessons I was given in the arts of divination, but there was no unseeing, unknowing, once the door was flung open.

One person may see a bird, while another sees the letter V in the same spot.

With the handle pointing toward you, as it represents you at this moment in time. Begin there and read clockwise, just like the hands on a clock,

Mentally divide the cup into three sections: rim, middle and base.

Step 6: The Reading.

Translating the symbols into meanings will vary per person, but most symbols are universal. For example, the letter "N" might bring to mind your friends name beginning with that letter rather than an answer of no to your question. Always go with the meaning that comes to mind first when interpreting the leaf patterns.

- The first symbol you saw represents your dominant character or someone near or influential in your life.
- Symbols in the rim section apply to this current period in time.
- The middle section represents the near future of the situation or question.
- Both the rim and middle section of the cup represent influences on the outcome as well as time placement.
- The base of your cup represents the ultimate answer to your question or conclusion to an event in question.

Wax Casting

Carromancy is one of the oldest types of divination, and again was taught to me by my German grandparents and my father, as he was taught by his grandfather. I remember from the time I was about four years old, my father sitting me in front of the fireplace for what seemed like forever to me then instructing me to control the flames. That to control the flames with my mind was important. Then the controlled flames would melt the wax and the water we pour it in is like a blank page for images, symbols and signs to appear to us and answer our questions. Like tea leaf or coffee ground reading, you are looking for symbols and little pictures to puzzle together a general reading or answer to a specific question. Unlike my father and others,

I don't like the water viewing method. So, I decided on using very heavy black card stock 8.5x11inches. I like it because it gives a nice big canvas for viewing, and if I am pouring for a client, they can take the wax casting home with them and it really cements the information brought forth through this form of divination.

I always say, you should get the same information giving a psychic, wax casting, tea leaf or card reading. They may garner a little extra information here or there, but it should all be versions of the same story. A truth is a truth no matter where it comes from.

You can use candle magic for many applications. You would use different colors of wax and sometimes additives to boost your results. In this experiment listed here I used additives to note any possible added benefits. I use red or pink for love, green or gold for cash, brown or yellow for questions regarding the home. Purple for spiritual questions. Blue and green for mind, body, intellectual questions. There are many varied answers to what color wax to use. Try different ones and see what connects for you. I also blend colors many times. This is all about connecting with your higher self to answer your questions or those of others and finding the tool you prefer and how you get the best results with each tool.

These were done using tea light size candles.
Photos of the pours will be at the end of the book.

Experiment 1:

Determine melting speed at various conditions, Ability to handle when melted, initial casting methods, how long candle can sit melted before the wax begins to be used up. Using black cardstock 110lb paper.

Experiment 2:

3 candles melted in same way as experiment 1 but before casting melted wax onto canvas this time, I hold the canvas over the candle to get smoke divination added to the reading.

Experiment 3:

Glitter added to candle #1 and #2, tea added to candle #3 and #4, then Cast #1 and #2 onto smoked canvas and #3 and #4 cast onto black cardstock.

Experiment 1

- 3 Candles numbered and lit at the same time
- 3 minutes in I added tablespoon of tea to candle #2
- I will add tea to candle #3 after completely melted to see if there is and difference in the cast
- Candle #2 is half melted at 12 minutes... candles #1 and #3 are 1/3melted (Does adding tea in some way speed the melting?
- 30 minutes in, candle #1 is melting faster than candle #2 or #3
- (#1 at 80%, #2 70#, #3 40%) Using the middle line in the candle as a 50% marker
- **#1 completely melted at 45 minutes.** I poured it immediately in a circular motion and it dries almost immediately and is easily seen. I was not surprised it made the shape of a skull as I am researching the dead and writing Spirited Tales Ghost Story Anthology. It looks like a bat flying down which means the spirits are speaking to me sending me the messages/ information I desire. The skull is not angry. It almost looks happy. I believe it confirms my thought they are happy about me writing and my Memento Mori collecting and that book. I especially feel their excitement for me to be doing these wax castings. The wick fell out as I poured facing up, meaning this will be very profitable, fun and so will the book. A shape of a hand to the left of the picture with a finger pointing up towards the third eye shows increased psychic abilities and heightened intuition. The single point at the top of the picture indicates for now I am on the right path staying single. I have

work to do and words to spread. If I wasn't a writer, I would tell the sitter to do so.

- At 51 minutes' candle #2 is at 90%, candle #3 is 70%.

At **1 hour 8 minutes candle #2 is melted completely.** Poured in the same circular manner it shows a child in the womb and a smaller one beside that but not the same womb, and not yet formed (conceived). Meaning: As I am the querent, it speaks to me as the center of its answers. I have been writing about and healing my inner child/childhood. It is the center of the casting and correctly has been central to my thoughts over the past several weeks creeping in even when doing something else. It is insisting on its truth being honored and told. The unformed child I believe, and feel is the yet unborn child of another female I know. I was visited by a young male spirit last week when brushing my teeth. He was very sweet and pretended to brush along with me. He mentally relayed he just wanted to introduce himself and was so excited he would be joining us in life soon.

The wick came apart in this casting falling in several places. The wick itself is lighting the way for me (my soul, self, inner child, inner voice etc.) It is also a sign of receiving help from others. The tea leaves trailing behind in mass show many harms done to the querent in the past from multiple people. One parent below the metal wick base pointing up representing the other parent the mother showing both are dead and in equal blame requesting forgiveness to move on in their spiritual lives.

There is a bar of gold behind my head to the back of the wax edge with a wax dot on each side representing my two children.

The two wax circles beneath the separating line between my womb and the unborn separate womb child shows I carried two children and will have one grandchild represented in a wax line or bloodline from the one child of mine.

The line of gold dots flowing from me beginning as a dot at my throat area in the womb, shows my voice, influence, work/writing will flow to many and for many years for a long lifetime.

Osteomancy or as my brother Bruce called it, throwing the bones, is a very ancient form of divination. Thousands of years old. Each bone represents something different to the reader. As the bones are tossed and fall in different directions or on top of one another, the diviner depending on what traditions and culture they learned in will work out the symbolism and the answer to the question posed.

Nephomancy or seeing shapes in clouds, is another childhood technique taught to me by my father. We would lay in the grass and watch the clouds looking for messages, letters, animals and more. This like several others I have listed, consist of looking for then interpreting those shapes or letters as messages from the universe to assist you in your life.

I know many will be disappointed there is no teaching on **Tarot**. That is a very lengthy and involved teaching to do it justice. I will be teaching more about this in a separate book devoted just to the history and different decks, and layouts. I have many rare and one of a kind antique handmade decks, as well as my own decks coming out next year, so you will definitely hear more about this subject in the near future.

ANGELS OF LIGHT

One of my favorite Angel prayers is short and simple:

> Angel of God, my guardian dear,
> To whom God's love commits me here,
> Ever this day or night be at my side,
> To light and guard, to rule and guide.
> Amen.

We humans possess what is commonly termed, "The Universal Law of Free Will," angels and archangels cannot intervene in our lives unless we ask them to help us. They are bound to stand by and watch even the most horrible scenes play out without intervening. The only exception to this rule, is if a life-endangering situation happens, where we would die before our time. Other than that extreme circumstance, we must remember to constantly invite angels and archangels into our lives.

Why are we burdened with a law that seems to stand in the way of getting assistance when we need it, without our asking? I believe it is, so we learn our lessons, and grow spirituality. To do this, we must experience the consequence of our choices, good and bad.

Many people ask me, "Do people who have died become angels?" Although some movies and books show this happening, I must say no.

Angels are created beings. They are a separate entity from humans and have never been human. When a human dies, I believe the soul, or life force leaves the body it has used on earth, then transition to embrace their true spirit form, hopefully going to heaven without any delay.

The Catholic belief system makes it clear we can and should pray to angels. Their belief is that in one example, Jesus himself warned us not to offend small children, because their guardian angels have guaranteed intercessory access to the Father. In Matthew 18:10 (NIV) it says, *"See that you do not despise one of these little ones; for I tell you that in heaven their angels always see the face of my Father who is in heaven"*

In the book of Revelation, angels are shown bringing the prayers of God's people. In the Revelation passages 8:3-4(NIV) they say, *"An angel came and stood at the altar in heaven with a golden censer; and he was given much incense to mingle with the prayers of all the saints upon the golden altar before the throne; and the smoke of the incense rose with the prayers of the saints from the hand of the angel before God."*

I believe you can think of and ask anyone living or dead to assist you in your prayers or petitions to God. You do not have to pray to them or saints with the thought they have power of their own to grant your requests. Rather you can bring them into your request as a helpmate on your behalf. We can ask them to pray with us to God, just as I could ask you to pray with me to God.

I have always like Bible verse, Matthew 18:20 (NIV) that says, For where two or three gathers in my name, there am I with them."

I hope by reading this book, you will learn different ways to tell the difference in who is connecting with you, and that you can safely interact with the unseen world through prayer and discernment.

If you reach out to your good angels, how will you know they are reaching back? Angels usually communicate directly. Everyone can perceive them, but just like everyone is psychic, we are all at different levels.

I think of our perceptive, or psychic, abilities like musical instruments. We and sound vibrate on multiple levels and frequencies. Some people are natural musicians. My father for instance, could play the violin and piano, from childhood, by ear, without ever having a lesson. I needed lessons, and never played to his level, even after many years of being taught.

Angels are in some varying levels of vibration, but all are higher than our normal human frequency. We need to raise our frequencies for two reasons: one, to steer clear of the lower lever dark forces that are all too happy to deceive us with messages that may well be true, but they are coming from a source you do not want to become friends with.

Second, the higher our frequencies, the easier it is for good angels to communicate with us by appearing to us in some form, or giving us a sign, or inspiring us and influencing us.

You might be drawn repeatedly to a certain place, or a book seems to just jump out at you that contains some form of message you need to receive.

Feathers and coins are two of their favorite ways to show you they are around you and hear what you say. You might find feathers or coins in very strange places as a way for them to say, "Hello, I'm with you!"

Angels are communicators and messengers. They work with your higher consciousness, or higher self, to relay those messages. It is your connection to the heavens and God, or a higher source or power depending on your belief system. Your Higher Self acts as a filter, so when you decide to open yourself to new teachings, or messages of inspiration, you can command your higher part of yourself to allow only that which is in your highest, greatest good to come to you, align with your soul's purpose, and assist you in every area of your life.

We do not always feel like angels are listening to our pleas, when in fact, they are always listening and trying to communicate as best they can, depending on our abilities and comfort levels with receiving the information. You do not have to chant anything special to the angels or do any special ceremonies when you want to create a closer relationship with your angels. Just talk to them.

Angels of all different realms are standing near you, ready to hear your questions and pleas. They will answer you, but you have got to pay attention. It could be an answer coming to you when you hear the same song repeatedly, or see number sequences, or words that keep repeating in your mind. Different angels that make up different realms oversee all the many parts of us and our lives that we could ever need their attention on. Just start asking. I believe angels cannot intervene, or assist us if we do not ask, because we have free will. If their assistance does not interfere with our life path, then I feel they not only come to our aid but want to be helpful to us as well.

Anytime you wish to open up to the spirit world, always do my favorite white light of protection around yourself: Take a deep breath, imagine in your mind, a brilliant pure white light coming down from above (I imagine God is sending down His protection from above) and it enters through the top of your head, and flows all through your body, until you are totally filled with the protective white light, running through the top of your head through the bottom of your feet running down through Mother Earth, as if you have roots like a tree coming from the bottoms of your feet. Imagine any negative feelings, any negative energies, or illness is cleansed out of your body by this light and leaving through the bottoms of your feet to be absorbed and changed once in the earth. Anything negative or hurtful is no longer with you.

Next, extend the light from inside of you to outside of you and fill your space with it. You can extend it out as far as you wish. Imagine, if you want, that you are surrounding your home, and vehicles, your workplace, and your loved ones with this beautiful protective light. Know that you and they are protected. This is something I do all the time. Especially first thing in the morning so I am assured my day will go as smoothly as possible.

The Christian description of the Angelic Realms is what we will be working with in this book. There are many other lists of realms if you research, depending on religion, or personal beliefs. Some think there are nine, or more different realms. Others believe the levels and combinations of angelic realms, and job descriptions, are endless. Honestly, I believe in many ways they are all correct. We can only give our best guess at what truly lies beyond. We will never know with 100 percent accuracy until we experience it ourselves when we die.

The first realm of Angels are the Seraphim, Cherubim and Thrones. They serve as the heavenly servants to God. Only Cherubim and Seraphim are represented with wings, Ezekiel 10:5. Seraphim are the highest angelic class. They serve as the caretakers of God's throne and continuously sing and shout praises to Him. In the Jewish faith, the Seraphim are said to be the highest rank of angel. This is probably because of their very proximity to God. Seraphim are sometimes called "the angels of love" because their name is the Hebrew root for "love." They are only mentioned in the Bible once in Isaiah, when he is being commissioned by God to be a prophet and he has a vision of heaven:

> Isaiah 6:1-7 King James Version (KJV), *In the year that king Uzziah died I saw also the Lord sitting upon a throne, high and lifted, and his train filled the temple.*
>
> *2 Above it stood the seraphim: each one had six wings; with twain, he covered his face, and with twain he covered his feet, and with twain he did fly.*
>
> *3 And one cried unto another, and said, Holy, holy, holy, is the Lord of hosts: the whole earth is full of his glory.*
>
> *4 And the posts of the door moved at the voice of him that cried, and the house was filled with smoke.*
>
> *5 Then said I, Woe is me! for I am undone; because I am a man of unclean lips, and I dwell during a people of unclean lips: for mine eyes, have seen the King, the Lord of hosts.*

6 Then flew one of the seraphim unto me, having a live coal in his hand, which he had taken with the tongs from off the altar:

7 And he laid it upon my mouth, and said, Lo, this hath touched thy lips; and thine iniquity is taken away, and thy sin purged.

Cherubim have four faces: one of a man, an ox, a lion, and an eagle. They have four conjoined wings covered with eyes, a lion's body figure, and they have ox's feet. Cherubim guard the way to the tree of life in the Garden of Eden, and guard God's Holy domain and presence from any sin and corruption.

When you mention Cherubim angels to people, the first image that pops into their mind is of the baby like angels floating on clouds, making love matches, or holding a harp. This is not the Cherubim of the Bible that I have read about. Cherubim are mentioned twice in Genesis and Ezekiel. In both instances, they are fierce protectors you do not want to mess with. They are all business. Not a harp or fluffy cloud anywhere in sight.

Genesis 3:22 (NAS), 22 *Then the LORD God said, "Behold, the man has become like one of Us, knowing good and evil; and now, he might stretch out his hand, and take also from the tree of life, and eat, and live forever" 23 therefore the LORD God sent him out from the garden of Eden, to cultivate the ground from which he was taken. 24 So He drove the man out; and at the east of the garden of Eden He stationed the cherubim and the flaming sword which turned every direction to guard the way to the tree of life.*

Ezekiel 1: 1-14 (NIV), 1In my thirtieth year, in the fourth month on the fifth day, while I was among the exiles by the Kebar River, the heavens were opened, and I saw visions of God.

2 On the fifth of the month—it was the fifth year of the exile of King Jehoiachin.

3 the word of the Lord came to Ezekiel the priest, the son of Buzi, by the Kebar River in the land of the Babylonians. There the hand of the Lord was on him.

4 I looked, and I saw a windstorm coming out of the north—an immense cloud with flashing lightning and surrounded by brilliant light. The center of the fire looked like glowing metal, 5 and in the fire, was what looked like four living creatures. In appearance, their form was human, 6 but each of them had four faces and four wings. 7 Their legs were straight; their feet were like those of a calf and gleamed like burnished bronze. 8 Under their wings on their four sides they had human hands. All four of them had faces and wings, 9 and the wings of one touched the wings of another. Each one went straight ahead; they did not turn as they moved.

10 Their faces looked like this: Each of the four had the face of a human being, and on the right side each had the face of a lion, and on the left the face of an ox; each also had the face of an eagle.

11 Such were their faces. They each had two wings spreading out upward, each wing touching that of the creature on either side; and each had two other wings covering its body.

12 Each one went straight ahead. Wherever the spirit would go, they would go, without turning as they went.

13 The appearance of the living creatures was like burning coals of fire or like torches. Fire moved back and forth among the creatures; it was bright, and lightning flashed out of it.

14 The creatures sped back and forth like flashes of lightning.

15 As I looked at the living creatures, I saw a wheel on the ground beside each creature with its four faces.

16 This was the appearance and structure of the wheels: They sparkled like topaz, and all four looked alike. Each appeared to be made like a wheel intersecting a wheel.

17 As they moved, they would go in any one of the four directions the creatures faced; the wheels did not change direction as the creatures went.

18 Their rims were high and awesome, and all four rims were full of eyes all around.

19 When the living creatures moved, the wheels beside them moved; and when the living creatures rose from the ground, the wheels also rose.

20 Wherever the spirit would go, they would go, and the wheels would rise along with them, because the spirit of the living creatures was in the wheels.

21 When the creatures moved, they also moved; when the creatures stood still, they also stood still; and when the creatures rose from the ground, the wheels rose along with them, because the spirit of the living creatures was in the wheels.

22 Spread out above the heads of the living creatures was what looked something like a vault, sparkling like crystal, and awesome.

23 Under the vault their wings were stretched out one toward the other, and each had two wings covering its body.

24 When the creatures moved, I heard their wings, like the roar of rushing waters, like the voice of the Almighty, like the tumult of an army. When they stood still, they lowered their wings.

25 Then there came a voice from above the vault over their heads as they stood with lowered wings.

26 Above the vault over their heads was what looked like a throne of lapis lazuli, and high above on the throne was a figure like that of a man.

27 I saw that from what appeared to be his waist up he looked like glowing metal, as if full of fire, and that from there down he looked like fire; and brilliant light surrounded him.

28 Like the appearance of a rainbow in the clouds on a rainy day, so was the radiance around him.

This was the appearance of the likeness of the glory of the Lord. When I saw it, I fell facedown, and I heard the voice of one speaking.

Ezekiel 10:3-8 (NIV), 1 Then I looked, and behold, in the expanse that was over the heads of the cherubim something like a sapphire stone, in appearance resembling a throne, appeared above them.

2 And He spoke to the man clothed in linen and said, "Enter between the whirling wheels under the cherubim and fill your hands with coals of fire from between the cherubim and scatter them over the city." And he entered in my sight.

3 Now the cherubim were standing on the right side of the temple when the man entered, and the cloud filled the inner court.

4 Then the glory of the LORD went up from the cherub to the threshold of the temple, and the temple was filled with the cloud and the court was filled with the brightness of the glory of the LORD.

5 Moreover, the sound of the wings of the cherubim was heard as far as the outer court, like the voice of God Almighty when He speaks.

6 It came about when He commanded the man clothed in linen, saying, "Take fire from between the whirling wheels, from between the cherubim," he entered and stood beside a wheel.

7 Then the cherub stretched out his hand from between the cherubim to the fire, which was between the cherubim, took some and put it into the hands of the one clothed in linen, who took it and went out.

8 The cherubim appeared to have the form of a man's hand under their wings.

9 Then I looked, and behold, four wheels beside the cherubim, one wheel beside each cherub; and the appearance of the wheels was like the gleam of a Tarshish stone.

10 As for their appearance, all four of them had the same likeness, as if one wheel were within another wheel.

11 When they moved, they went in any of their four directions without turning as they went; but they followed in the direction which they faced, without turning as they went.

12 Their whole body, their backs, their hands, their wings and the wheels were full of eyes all around, the wheels belonging to all four of them.

13 The wheels were called in my hearing, the whirling wheels.

14 And each one had four faces. The first face was the face of a cherub, the second face was the face of a man, the third the face of a lion, and the fourth the face of an eagle.

15 Then the cherubim rose. They are the living beings that I saw by the river Chebar.

16 Now when the cherubim moved, the wheels would go beside them; also, when the cherubim lifted their wings to rise from the ground, the wheels would not turn from beside them.

17 When the cherubim stood still, the wheels would stand still; and when they rose, the wheels would rise with them, for the spirit of the living beings was in them.

18 Then the glory of the LORD departed from the threshold of the temple and stood over the cherubim.

19 When the cherubim departed, they lifted their wings and rose from the earth in my sight with the wheels beside them; and they stood still at the entrance of the east gate of the LORD'S house, and the glory of the God of Israel hovered over them.

20 These are the living beings that I saw beneath the God of Israel by the river Chebar; so, I knew that they were cherubim.

21 Each one had four faces and each one four wings, and beneath their wings was the form of human hands.

22 As for the likeness of their faces, they were the same faces whose appearance I had seen by the river Chebar. Each one went straight ahead.

Another instance, where movies use biblical accounts in their onscreen stories is, "Indiana Jones and the Raiders of the Lost Ark." Indiana Jones is battling against a group of Nazis who are searching for the Ark of the Covenant, which Adolf Hitler believed would make his army invincible.

The Bible describes Cherubim in the construction of the 'Ark of the Covenant'. The Ark was the dwelling place of God with the Israelites during their exodus in the desert.

Exodus 25:17-22 (NLT), 10 *"Have the people make an Ark of acacia wood—a sacred chest 45 inches*

17 "Then make the Ark's cover—the place of atonement—from pure gold. It must be 45 inches long and 27 inches wide.

18 Then make two cherubim from hammered gold and place them on the two ends of the atonement cover.

19 Mold the cherubim on each end of the atonement cover, making it all of one piece of gold.

20 The cherubim will face each other and look down on the atonement cover. With their wings spread above it, they will protect it.

21 Place inside the Ark the stone tablets inscribed with the terms of the covenant, which I will give to you. Then put the atonement cover on top of the Ark.

22 I will meet with you there and talk to you from above the atonement cover between the gold cherubim that hover over the Ark of the Covenant. From there I will give you my commands for the people of Israel.

Thrones are living symbols of God's justice and authority and have as one of their symbols the throne. They are in the part of the realm where material form begins to take shape. The lower realms of angels need the Thrones to access God. Thrones by some are thought to be the twenty-four elder men who listen to the will of God and present the prayers of men, are mentioned in the book of revelation.

In Kabbalah, the thrones are led by Archangel Raziel, meaning wisdom.

The second realm of angels, work as heavenly managers, guiding and ruling the spirits. Dominions regulate the duties of the lower level angels. The Dominions are believed to look like beautiful humans, with a pair of feathered wings. They carry out God's wishes. Only very rarely will they make themselves physically known to humans but are responsible for answering prayers in many instances. Two Dominions were the angels from the story of Sodom and Gomorrah. Genesis 19 (HCSB), The Destruction of Sodom and Gomorrah

1 The two angels entered Sodom in the evening as Lot was sitting at Sodom's •gate. When Lot saw them, he got up to meet them. He bowed with his face to the ground

2 and said, "My lords, turn aside to your servant's house, wash your feet, and spend the night. Then you can get up early and go on your way." "No," they said. "We would rather spend the night in the square."

3 But he urged them so strongly that they followed him and went into his house. He prepared a feast and baked unleavened bread for them, and they ate.

4 Before they went to bed, the men of the city of Sodom, both young and old, the whole population, surrounded the house.

5 They called out to Lot and said, "Where are the men who came to you tonight? Send them out to us so we can have sex with them!"

6 Lot went out to them at the entrance and shut the door behind him.

7 He said, "Don't do this evil, my brothers.

8 Look, I've got two daughters who haven't had sexual relations with a man I'll bring them out to you, and you can do whatever you want to them. However, don't do anything to these men, because they have come under the protection of my roof."

9 "Get out of the way!", They said, adding, "This one came here as a foreigner, but he's acting like a judge! Now we'll do more harm to you than to them." They put pressure on Lot and came up to break down the door.

10 But the angels reached out, brought Lot into the house with them, and shut the door.

11 They struck the men who were at the entrance of the house, both young and old, with a blinding light so that they were unable to find the entrance.

12 Then the angels said to Lot, "Do you have anyone else here: a son-in-law, your sons and daughters, or anyone else in the city who belongs to you? Get them out of this place,

13 for we are about to destroy this place because the outcry against its people is so great before the LORD, that the LORD has sent us to destroy it."

14 So Lot went out and spoke to his sons-in-law, who were going to marry his daughters. "Get up," he said. "Get out of this place, for the LORD is about to destroy the city!" But his sons-in-law thought he was joking.

15 At daybreak the angels urged Lot on: "Get up! Take your wife and your two daughters who are here, or you will be swept away in the punishment of the city."

16 But he hesitated. Because of the LORD's compassion for him, the men grabbed his hand, his wife's hand, and the hands of his two daughters. Then they brought him out and left him outside the city.

17 As soon as the angels got them outside, one of them said, "Run for your lives! Don't look back and don't stop anywhere on the plain! Run to the mountains, or you will be swept away!"

18 But Lot said to them, "No, my lords please.

19 Your servant has indeed found favor in your sight, and you have shown me great kindness by saving my life. But I can't run to the mountains; the disaster will overtake me, and I will die.

20 Look, this town is close enough for me to run to. It is a small place. Please let me go there — it's only a small place, isn't it? — so that I can survive."

21 And he said to him, "All right, I'll grant your request about this matter too and will not demolish the town you mentioned.

22 Hurry up! Run there, for I cannot do anything until you get there." Therefore, the name of the city is Zoar.

23 The sun had risen over the land when Lot reached Zoar.

24 Then out of the sky the LORD rained burning sulfur on Sodom and Gomorrah from the LORD.

25 He demolished these cities, the entire plain, all the inhabitants of the cities, and whatever grew on the ground.

26 But his wife looked back and became a pillar of salt.

27 Early in the morning Abraham went to the place where he had stood before the LORD.

28 He looked down toward Sodom and Gomorrah and all the land of the plain, and he saw that smoke was going up from the land like the smoke of a furnace.

29 So it was, when God destroyed the cities of the plain, He remembered Abraham and brought Lot out of the middle of the upheaval when He demolished the cities where Lot had lived.

Virtues are the angels through which, signs and miracles are seen, and made in the world. In Acts 27:23-25 (NIV), St. Paul tells the men on his ship: *"Last night an angel of the God to whom I belong and whom I serve stood beside me and said, 'Do not be afraid, Paul. You must stand trial before Caesar; and God has graciously given you the lives of all who sail with you.' So, keep up your courage, men, for I have faith in God that it will happen just as he told me."* The virtue angel's prophecy of the future came true. All 276 of the men on the ship survived the wreck, and Paul later faced Caesar on trial.

The Jewish and Christian apocryphal, The Life of Adam and Eve describes a group of angels accompanying Archangel Michael to encourage Eve, while she gave birth. Two virtue angels were among the group; one stood by Eve's left side and on her right.

Acts 1:10-11, tells of virtue angels at the ascension to heaven of the resurrected Jesus Christ.

Powers are the warrior angels, who oppose evil spirits. They are usually represented as soldiers, wearing full armor and helmets. Carrying weapons such as shields, spears or chains. The main purpose of the Powers is to keep the balance of power in the favor of the light, or positive realm. They are sometimes referred to as the angels of birth and death.

The third realm angels, function as heavenly guides, protectors, and messengers to human beings. Principalities, Inspire artists, scientists and inventors. They carry out the orders given to them by the upper sphere angels and bring blessings to the world in material form. Their task is to oversee groups of people. They are the educators and guardians of the realm of earth.

Messenger Angels, the lowest order of angels, and the most recognized. They are the ones most concerned with the affairs of living things. They have many different functions in this realm. The angels are sent as messengers to humanity. Personal guardian angels come from this class.

Personal, guardian angels, are not their own order but rather all come from the lowest order, the Angels. It is a common belief that they are assigned to every human being, whether Christian or not. George Washington spoke openly of his visions, and conversations with his Guardian Angel, and credited the success at Valley Forge to "an inspiring visit from a heavenly being." President Abraham Lincoln stated that he often called upon the wisdom of the Angels to help him lead the country during very trying times.

Ask for a list of Archangels and you will get varied answers depending on a person's faith. Most agree that seven archangels supervise other Angels, specializing in different types of work helping humanity, and four of those are considered by many to be the most important archangels of all. Their names are Michael, Gabriel, Raphael, and Uriel.

The earliest reference to the seven archangels as a group appears in the Book of Enoch. Although not part of the Jewish Canon, it is part of the Judaic tradition, where the seven Archangels are listed as, Michael, Gabriel, Raphael, Sariel, Uriel, Remiel and Raguel. They are called Messengers.

Zoroastrianism, an ancient religion started a thousand years before the birth of Christ, believed in light beings or Fravashi, that manifested the energy of the Divine. They believed that each person had at least one Fravashi, the same way we view guardian angels.

Islamic faith acknowledges four Archangels. Angels are mentioned repeatedly in both the Koran and the Hadith, speaking of them as faithful servants of Allah. Jibreel or Gabriel, who communicates Allah's words to His prophets. Israfeel or Raphael, who will blow the trumpet to mark the Day of Judgment. Mikail or Michael, believed to oversee rainfall and substance. Munkar and Nakeer, who after death, question souls in the grave about their works of faith and what they did in life. Malak Am-Maut, the Angel of Death, who after death captures the soul of the dead person. Malik, the guardian of hell, and Ridwan, the guardian of heaven. There are other unnamed angels who carry Allah's throne, act as guardians and protectors of believers, and those who record a person's good and bad deeds.

Even people who identify as non-religious, spiritual, agnostic or atheistic, speak of their belief in the presence and intervention of angels in human life. They refer to them at times as spirit guides or guardian spirits in their lives. Angels are, in some way, a part of almost every person's personal belief system.

Here are four of the most commonly agreed upon Archangels:

Michael is the only angel mentioned by name in all three major sacred texts of the world's religions. The Torah (Judaism), the Bible (Christianity), and the Qur'an (Islam). Michael a leading angel who fights evil, the leader of all archangels, and the one now, closest to God, after the fall of Lucifer. Revelation 12:7-9 (NIV),

7 Then war broke out in heaven. Michael and his angels fought against the dragon, and the dragon and his angels fought back.

8 But he was not strong enough, and they lost their place in heaven.

9 The great dragon was hurled down—that ancient serpent called the devil, or Satan, who leads the whole world astray. He was hurled to the earth, and his angels with him.

He is the angel of the South, and of the element of fire, He is a powerful protector from evil.

Michael is the most prayed to Archangel of them all. His ability to protect us from evil is the reason he is prayed to by many paranormal investigators around the world.

Gabriel has always been my favorite Archangel. He rules over the direction west, and the element of water and inspires people to create change in themselves and be receptive to God and his teachings. Gabriel is the angel of revelation because God often uses Gabriel to deliver the most important messages to people. Maybe his most important message was when he visited a young Virgin Mary to foretell her future as Jesus Christ's mother on Earth. Luke 1:29, God sent the angel Gabriel to Nazareth, a village in Galilee,

27 to a virgin named Mary. She was engaged to be married to a man named Joseph, a descendant of King David.

28 Gabriel appeared to her and said, "Greetings, favored woman! The Lord is with you!"

29 Confused and disturbed, Mary tried to think what the angel could mean.

30 "Don't be afraid, Mary," the angel told her, "for you have found favor with God!

31 You will conceive and give birth to a son, and you will name him Jesus.

32 He will be very great and will be called the Son of the Highest. The Lord God will give him the throne of his ancestor David.

33 And he will reign over Israel forever; his Kingdom will never end!"

34 Mary asked the angel, "But how can this happen? I am a virgin."

35 The angel replied, "The Holy Spirit will come upon you, and the power of the Highest will overshadow you. So, the baby to be born will be holy, and he will be called the Son of God.

36 What's more, your relative Elizabeth has become pregnant in her old age! People used to say she was barren, but she has conceived a son and is now in her sixth month.

37 For nothing is impossible with God."

38 Mary responded, "I am the Lord's servant. May everything you have said about me come true." And then the angel left her.

Raphael is the Angel of the east, and the element air. His job is to help you realize you are never alone, and to cast your cares to God to handle. Raphael is the Archangel of healing. He will assist you and heal you unless your illness or death is part of the divine plan for your life here on earth. Raphael will put the right doctors or healers, and medicines in your path, and is known for bringing miraculous healings to people. Relationships of all kinds, are also his territory to assist, restore, and bring harmony to. He is the protector of the earth and will often make his presence known to you in nature settings.

Uriel is angel of the north and the element of earth. As the angel of earth, Uriel grounds people in God's wisdom, working to give you practical solutions for your problems. Working closely with Archangel Raphael, they are guardians of birds, fish and all manner of wildlife and the environment. Uriel is often depicted carrying either a book or a scroll, both of which represent wisdom. Another symbol connected with Uriel is an open hand holding a flame, which represents God's truth.

Uriel gives prophetic information and warnings. For example, Uriel warned Noah of the impending flood, helped the prophet Ezra to interpret mystical predictions about the forthcoming Messiah. In several Christian apocryphal gospels, Uriel rescues John the Baptist in the time of Jesus birth, when King Herod's order to round up and kill young males. Uriel takes John, his mother Elizabeth to join Jesus and his parents in Egypt. In Jewish tradition, Uriel is the one who checked the doors of homes throughout Egypt for lamb's blood, which representing faithfulness to God during Passover's deadly plague striking down first-born children as a judgment for sin, sparing children of the faithful.

Angels, not surprisingly, are mentioned almost 300 times in the Bible!

Hebrews 13:2 (New King James Version) reminds us, 2 Be not forgetful to entertain strangers: for thereby some have entertained angels unawares.

How do you know if you are entertaining, conversing with, and taking the advice of a good angel, versus a dark, or fallen angel?

Honestly, it's not that easy sometimes. Many well-intentioned people have fallen prey to dark forces pretending to be light, helpful spirits, or angels. You can't assume that behind every smile lays the wish only to see your highest and greatest good achieved.

We have all heard stories, or seen cartoons and commercials showing the good angel on one shoulder urging you to do the right thing, while the bad angel sits on the other shoulder telling you all the reasons you should do something based on what makes you feel best, what you want, without any thought of consequences or the well-being of others.

Part of discerning or having spiritual insight into the plans and purposes of good versus evil, is trusting your feelings. This ability becomes instantaneous or second nature the better you know yourself. Learning to trust that gut feeling, tied to your higher consciousness and intuition, will be the best lie detector.

I believe spending time in nature, walking through the park, tending your garden, watching the clouds float by, are excellent moments to have that quiet time to reflect or meditate, clear your mind, and raise your vibration to operate in the realm of clarity. We all get so caught up in the business of life we forget sometimes to connect with a very important person: ourselves.

There are many who believe that all the so called "New Age beliefs" are merely an excellent deception to make God's followers fall into practices that are nothing more than sorcery tricks of Satan, packaged as enlightenment from God. Others will tell you this itself is nonsense, perpetuated to make you fall in line with a controlling religious group.

Which is it? I am not here to tell you what to believe. You must make your own decision based on your personal feelings on the matter. I will tell you that when dealing with good angels, you will be better for the encounter. They are helpful, loving beings who want nothing from you. They will never say, "You will be granted your desire if..." They are messengers of light who will never threaten or harm you. They only want to see you safe and happy.

So, if you feel negative emotions, feel you must do something they want in return to grant your request, then you are not dealing with a good angel.

There is so much confusion about whether good angels speak to us in dreams or visions. I believe they do. That may be given to us awake or asleep in the form of inspiration, hope, or a vision. You should keep a notebook or journal by your bedside to record the messages they give you, or dreams you believe to be Important. You may think you could not possibly forget a special message from your angel, or dream where they appeared to you, but it happens to people all the time.

The Bible speaks of receiving a vision and understanding what the vision meant. Daniel 8:13-19; 9:21-23 (NIV) tells us,

13 Then I heard a holy one speaking, and another holy one said to him, "How long will it take for the vision to be fulfilled—the vision concerning the daily sacrifice, the rebellion that causes desolation, the surrender of the sanctuary and the trampling underfoot of the Lord's people?"

14 He said to me, "It will take 2,300 evenings and mornings; then the sanctuary will be reconsecrated."

15 While I, Daniel, was watching the vision and trying to understand it, there before me stood one who looked like a man.

16 And I heard a man's voice from the Ulai calling, "Gabriel, tell this man the meaning of the vision."

17 As he came near the place where I was standing, I was terrified and fell prostrate. "Son of man," he said to me, "understand that the vision concerns the time of the end."

18 While he was speaking to me, I was in a deep sleep, with my face to the ground. Then he touched me and raised me to my feet.

19 He said: "I am going to tell you what will happen later in the time of wrath, because the vision concerns the appointed time of the end. 20 The two-horned ram that you saw represents the kings of Media and Persia. 21 The shaggy goat is the king of Greece, and the large horn between its eyes is the first king. 22 The four horns that replaced the one that was broken off represent four kingdoms that will emerge from his nation but will not have the same power.

23 "In the latter part of their reign, when rebels have become completely wicked, a fierce-looking king, a master of intrigue, will arise. 24 He will become very strong, but not by his own power. He will cause astounding devastation and will succeed in whatever he does. He will destroy those who are mighty, the holy people. 25 He will cause deceit to prosper, and he will consider himself superior. When they feel secure, he will destroy many and take his stand against the Prince of princes. Yet he will be destroyed, but not by human power.

26 "The vision of the evenings and mornings that has been given you is true, but seal up the vision, for it concerns the distant future."

27 I, Daniel, was worn out. I lay exhausted for several days. Then I got up and went about the king's business. I was appalled by the vision; it was beyond understanding.

Angels will come to us in times of our greatest challenges in life. They want to support us, to give us comfort.

The night before his death by crucifixion, Jesus Christ went to the Garden of Gethsemane on the Mount of Olives outside of Jerusalem to pray, a good angel of comfort, Archangel Chamuel met Jesus there to encourage him at a very frightening time in his life.

Luke 22:41-43 (NIV): *"He withdrew about a stone's throw beyond them, knelt down and prayed, 'Father, if you are willing, take this cup from me; yet not my will, but yours be done.'" An angel from heaven appeared to him and strengthened him." Immediately after the angel strengthens Jesus, Jesus could pray "more earnestly," says Luke 22:44* (NIV): *"And being in anguish, he prayed more earnestly, and his sweat was like drops of blood falling to the ground."*

Some people wonder if it is possible that this happened. But, in fact, a high level of emotional agony can cause people to sweat blood. The condition is called Hematidrosis. This can occur when the sweat glands hemorrhage, then causing a person to sweat blood, or even cry tears of blood.

Jesus further mentions good angels that would immediately come to his aid if only he called on them, in Matthew 26:52-54 (NIV), in the passages describing the night the Roman soldiers arrive to arrest Jesus, and one of Jesus' disciples tries to defend Jesus by cutting off the ear of one of the Romans. Jesus says: *"'Put your sword back in its place, for all who draw the sword will die by the sword. Do you think I cannot call on my Father, and he will at once put at my disposal more than 12 legions of angels? But how then would the Scriptures be fulfilled that say it must happen in this way?"*

Good Angels give assistance when we need it, when we ask, if it does not interfere with the plan for our life here on earth. Your angels will step in and help you.

One of my favorite uplifting quotes that I keep where I can see it daily, is a Jewish proverb saying, "Every blade of grass has an angel bending over it saying, "Grow, Grow!" I think of this in the way we have Guiding Angels that help and assist us in every area of our lives.

Angelic help is unlimited. Angels are happy to help you without limit. When you ask for good angels to assist you, remember, you must believe and stay alert to receive the answers, or signs they are trying to give you.

Several studies and polls in the USA, taken by respondents of diverse religious faiths: evangelical Protestants, black Protestants, mainline Protestants, Catholics and Jews. discovered that more than half of all adults, including one in five of those who say they are not religious, believe they have been protected by a guardian angel during their life. Researchers found that a belief in guardian angels, affirmed sixty percent of respondents, is a phenomenon that crosses religious, as well as regional and educational lines. This holds true for Europeans as well, overall almost eight out of ten people polled in various studies, agreed with the statement that "there are things in life that we simply cannot explain through science or any other means."

Angels can help protect us physically as well as spiritually. There have been numerous stories, for example, of people being rescued from harmful situations by mysterious strangers who seem to depart just as suddenly as they first appeared! Are these unexplained messengers and helpers, angels?

Animals Encounter Angels

In the Bible, God reveals animal intelligence through the unusual encounter of Balaam with his donkey (Num. 22:21-33 (NIV). In that incident, the donkey saw the Angel of the Lord standing in the way and moved aside. Balaam became angry with the donkey because it wouldn't obey him. Yet the Angel of the Lord credited the donkey's quick thinking for Balaam's deliverance. He declared, "The donkey saw me and turned aside from me these three times. If she had not turned aside from me, I would surely have killed you" (v. 33). The donkey recognized the danger and made a decision to get out of the way of the Angel, whom Balaam couldn't even see.

The incident of Balaam and his donkey brings into focus another insight about animals. It reveals that it is possible for animals to see angels (Num. 22:21-33). In that incident, Balaam was spared death at the hands of the Angel of the Lord because Balaam's donkey "turned aside" when it saw the angel. The text does not say the Angel of the Lord revealed his presence to the donkey. It tells us simply that the donkey saw the Angel.

Humans see angels when the angels want to reveal themselves. The donkey saw the Angel of the Lord without his self-revelation. In fact, judging from the Angel's comments to Balaam (see v. 33), the donkey was actually acting contrary to the Angel's intentions.

Matthew 10:29 "Are not two sparrows sold for a penny? And not one of them will fall to the ground apart from your Father."

God values us above his creatures, but even a tiny sparrow,

which is valued at less than one penny to us, is still valuable to God, meaning that He cares for His creatures and cares deeply about how we treat them, regardless of how small or insignificant they are.

Psalm 50:10-11 (NIV) "For every beast of the forest is mine, the cattle on a thousand hills. I know all the birds of the hills, and all that moves in the field is mine."

DARKER ANGELS

I know from many years involved with the paranormal that certain signs and similarities occur when a lower level or dark energy is around. I have experienced the fast dying flowers, quickly rotting fruit, irregularly large numbers of flies in an area, foul odors (especially Sulphur), thriving fish in my aquarium suddenly dying end masse, and more. These are not good signs. Something is in your space that should not be there.

Despite knowing all this, I still do not jump to conclusions. I am a skeptical believer. People find this strange after so many encounters. Why don't I just believe without exception? Everyone has different personalities. I am just more skeptical; I think ninety nine percent of all phenomena can be explained in some way. Bad plumbing, old wiring, even many electric towers in the area can cause hallucinations. If I hear a bump in the night, my first thought is to check and see if someone is breaking into my house, not assume a spirit is around.

To me the only thing to be concerned with is that one percent. That's where all the questions and wonderment lie. One percent of totally unexplainable occurrences, now that should have your full attention, and keep you up at night.

Out of the one percent of truly unexplained occurrences, I believe only a very small part of those are truly demonic encounters. With the saturation of the paranormal and ghost investigations on television, radio, the internet, and in magazines, ghost hunters and interested seekers have grown desensitized, and perhaps a little bored with even the best examples of the unexplained. They want something more, so what's next up on the fear chart? Demons.

I don't know if it was just boredom, or if the ratings were slipping in some accounts, but there is now an influx of demons being conjured, called to, provoked and just plain made up. All of this playing to the insatiable audiences watching and reading the accounts. Now having said that, there is a percentage of those accounts that are in fact very real, probably to the surprise, and horror of some people involved.

Dark forces are all around us. No question about it. I just want you to be aware that not everything falls under this heading. At the same time, arm yourself with enough knowledge to be safe when they are encountered.

Malevolent Entities are created spirit beings living in the non-physical realm. They are their own kind, they were never human but will often pretend to be deceased loved ones or animals, but they especially love to appear to be children. This will lure you closer by feeling sorry for them or feeding on your natural instincts to lower your guard for a child. Dark energies are around us every bit as much as the light and you need to understand this balance of higher and lower vibrational energies you navigate through daily. There are some ways all spirits "show" themselves. Here are a few brief descriptions.

While it is rare to see a full apparition that appears to be a living person, it does happen.

Typical apparitions occur while you are awake, and they tend to be translucent. Many people have reported seeing animals or of non-human entities evil spirits act in direct opposition to "God" and good energy and can be fallen, angels. When a person is possessed, they are believed to be inhabited by a demon.

Imps can be traced to Germanic folklore where the imp is a small demon always bent on performing mischievous tricks on others. I have been surprised to hear how many people have been troubled by these lately.

Doppelgangers German folklore tells us is that people and living creatures have a twin in spirit form who although invisible, is identical to the living entity if ever they are seen. These other selves are not ghosts because that would only apply after death. These are with you during your living years. Believed by some to be evil or foretell of negative future happenings. German writer Johann Paul Richter wrote under the pseudonym, Jean Paul. In 1796, he coined the word Doppelgänger and used it in his writing.

The later life of French novelist and master of the short story Guy de Maupassant is particularly interesting to me as a writer who at times feels influenced or aided in my writing by unseen entities or forces good and bad. He claimed his book "The Horla," was dictated to him by his doppelganger that would walk into the room take a chair right in front of him speak to him. What was the book about? It is a terrifying tale of a man waking up to a ghost that is his evil spirit double sitting on his chest, slowly consuming his soul. Shortly after it was written, the tale is mirrored in his real life. Guy tried to commit suicide by cutting his throat. He was committed to the private asylum Esprit Blanche at Passy, in Paris, where he died July 1893. Guy De Maupassant penned his epitaph: "I have coveted everything and taken pleasure in nothing." He is buried in Section 26 of the Montparnasse Cemetery, Paris.

Throughout history, claims have been made by people saying they encountered apparitions of themselves or that they experienced the phenomenon of bilocation, which is being in two separate locations at the very same time.

Parasitic Entities drain the energy of their victims leaving them fatigued and weak. This also makes them more readily available to be influenced or used by negative forces for their gain or amusement. We all know people we call energy vampires, who after they leave our presence seem to have taken all our power with them. It is the same principal.

Poltergeists are evil entities that cause chaos and terror.

Poltergeists violently throw objects, open and close doors, pound on walls, or physically assault the living.

Shadow People are at times stationary but often are reported to be flashes of shadow or fast-moving gray matter. They are thought to be low vibrational and ill-intentioned energy.

Let's look at world views concerning demons and lower energy entities. Here are the biblical accounts. These are what most people, even non-religious, or non-believers are familiar with, having heard the stories possibly while growing up.

There are belief systems that do not believe evil is an entity at all, merely our fears and undeveloped higher selves expressing these fears in forms considered evil, or that we are told stories written by mere men used by the Church to control the masses.

I am not trying to lead you to believe any views stated here. I just want to enlighten you with what I have found through years of research, with some of those studies centered around my seminary work, leading to my ordination as a non-denominational minister in 2011.

The Bible takes Satan and demons seriously. In return, they know the Bible better than most any human on earth. Why? Because, in my opinion, they are at battle with the forces of good. And, like any war, the one who knows his enemy best has the advantage. Where do we fit in this battle? Right in the middle of the light and dark forces. Let's examine some reasons for my belief.

In the Bible, Jesus states many times that the dark forces are real and can and do cause harm to humans. Ephesians 6:12, (Berean Literal Bible) because to us the wrestling is not against blood and flesh, but against the rulers, against the authorities, against the cosmic powers of this darkness, against the spiritual forces of evil in the heavenly realms. There is no great concern over this, because the dark forces will fall in the end. Here are some passages relating to this battle of good versus evil, in case you are not familiar.

Jesus, who in the Bible, is savior to the world, is confronted after his Baptism by Satan. We are told in the Bible that Satan leads a massive army of darkness, meaning demons and other low-level energies. The devil and the demons are angelic beings who rebelled against God and were cast down. I believe the "down" is earth. I think that's why negative energy seems to move faster, and consume so many, so quickly on earth, versus good. Good, often appears to have to win a battle for a positive outcome.

Satan tempts Jesus three times in the following passages, to Worship the devil in return for all the kingdoms of the world, to relieve his hunger by turning stones into bread, and to Jump from a pinnacle and rely on angels to break his fall, to put doubt into Jesus as to if God would be manipulated, a perform if tested in this way.

> Luke 4:1-13 (KJV), 1 *And Jesus being full of the Holy Ghost returned from Jordan, and was led by the Spirit into the wilderness,*
>
> *2 Being forty days tempted of the devil. And in those days, he did eat nothing: and when they were ended, he afterward hungered.*
>
> *3 And the devil said unto him, if thou be the Son of God, command this stone that it be made bread.*
>
> *4 And Jesus answered him, saying, it is written, that man shall not live by bread alone, but by every word of God.*
>
> *5 And the devil, taking him up into a high mountain, shewed unto him all the kingdoms of the world in a moment of time.*
>
> *6 And the devil said unto him, all this power will I give thee, and the glory of them: for that is delivered unto me; and to whomsoever I will I give it.*
>
> *7 If thou therefore wilt worship me, all shall be thine.*
>
> *8 And Jesus answered and said unto him, get thee behind me, Satan: for it is written, thou shalt worship the Lord thy God, and him only shalt thou serve.*

9 And he brought him to Jerusalem, and set him on a pinnacle of the temple, and said unto him, if thou be the Son of God, cast thyself down from hence:

10 For it is written, He shall give his angels charge over thee, to keep thee:

11 And in their hands, they shall bear thee up, lest at any time thou dash thy foot against a stone.

12 And Jesus answering said unto him, it is said, thou shalt not tempt the Lord thy God.

13 And when the devil had ended all the temptation, he departed from him for a season. Then holy angels arrive to be with Jesus as he victoriously prepares to begin his public ministry work in the world.

The battle between good versus evil is not just a Christian battle of powers. If you study world religions, and mythologies, you will find many similar creation stories, and stories very much like the Christian story of Jesus. In Buddhism for example, Buddha battles the demon Mara, referred to as the Lord of Death. Like the temptation story of Jesus, Mara tempts Siddhartha. Mara brought his most beautiful daughters to seduce him, but he remained in meditation. Then, Mara sent armies of monsters to attack him, but he remained seated and unharmed. Mara as a final temptation, claimed that the seat of enlightenment rightfully belonged to him and not to the mortal Siddhartha. Mara's monstrous soldiers said, "We are his witnesses!" Mara challenged Siddhartha, who will speak for you? Siddhartha touched his right hand to the earth, and the earth said: "I bear you witness!" Mara vanished. Then the morning star rose in the sky, Siddhartha realized enlightenment and became a Buddha.

Most world cultures from ancient times to modern interpretations, feature the Devil or demons somewhere in their religion or mythology.

In several satanic cults, Satan represents an opposition to God, but to them, does not represent evil, just a battle for power.

In the middle ages, the Devil represented those that revolted against the insistence to become Christian. Several of today's symbols originate from this period. One example is the Trident. In medieval times, Pagan gods were demonized to discredit them in the eyes of their followers, hoping to gain more souls for the Christian Religion. The trident in ancient Greek and Hindu religions was a weapon against evil, but during these times was changed to represent a tool of the devil, and a weapon of evil to be used against the innocent.

Another example of how early Christianity discredited a pagan god was by giving horns to the devil. Horns were commonly known at that time to belong to a favorite symbol of the Celtic god Cernunnos.

There was a time the early Hebrews in the Old Testament, where God was it, there was no opposing evil, just God in the hot seat. Either praise him or blame him, for all things befalling humans. In, Isaiah 45:7 (NIV), *I form the light, and create darkness. I make peace and create calamity. I am Yahweh, who does all these things.*

Why do you have to have evil in the first place? Well, any religion that preaches redemption, must have an evil to overcome, to then move past, and be redeemed, or made new, "good", again.

The idea of a separate evil one was a gradual change through the ages. In the mid second century, the shift began to take hold. By that time, Enoch's influence can be seen in the New Testament. Although his writings are not included except in the Apocryphal. He is quoted by Jude in the bible. Verses 14-15 from the Book of Enoch, *"Enoch, the seventh from Adam, prophesied about these men: 'See, the Lord is coming with thousands upon thousands of his holy ones to judge everyone, and to convict all the ungodly of all the ungodly acts they have done in the ungodly way, and of all the harsh words ungodly sinners have spoken against him." Many believe this gives credence, that his works was prophetic, and should be included in the Bible, however that is unlikely to change at this point.*

The apocryphal contains some of my favorite writings. I believe so many people would better understand the environment of the times, how people lived, the belief systems and politics in place, when these books were written, if these had not been discarded from the Bible.

So exactly how do we begin to understand all the levels or shades of darkness? Well, we need to get clear on who's in charge. There are varying beliefs on who the evil one is, he is called by so many names, Prince of Darkness, The fallen Morning Star, Beelzebub, Samael, Lucifer, Satan and many more.

And who are his demon legion? Many believe that demons are Nephilim, the offspring of sexual relationships between the fallen sons of God, that after the battle in Heaven, were cast down with Lucifer, and they mated with the human daughters of the men on earth. Specifically, Incubi were thought to be demons who had sexual relations with women, sometimes producing a child by the woman. Succubae, by contrast, were demons thought to have intercourse with men.

What about the "terrible ones", the Rephaim Giants, who lived in Canaan and elsewhere at the time of Moses and Joshua? Are they the same as Nephilim? Yes, I believe so. The names are mixed in use, but I believe they are the same and not a separate species of giant, human-angel hybrid. They are spoken of in Old Testament, wreaking havoc on people, and spreading fear throughout the lands. The battle between Moses and the giant Amorite king Og, is described in detail in the book of Deuteronomy. If you research beginning there, you find that in Moses's time, Og was king over sixty fortified cities, all of which the Israelites ultimately captured. His bed was made of iron and to hold his over ten-foot-tall body, was 13.5 feet long by 6 feet wide.

While I do believe in giants, I do not feel they are demons.

They may have been terrifying, but I believe demons are a lower level than angels. Dark angels, I believe, either came down to earth, or were cast down, depending on the tale you accept. One difference between a demon and an angel is that demons seek a body to inhabit, while the more powerful angel can appear in bodily form.

I believe angels, even dark ones, are by nature of their creation, entities, with numerous powers they use with abandon. The leader of the dark angels is Satan. All other dark angels would fall under his authority, and demons below that. Demons are vast in number making up part of the dark army. They degrade the bodies they invade and possess, whether of animals or men. Demons are unclean in their minds and actions, deceiving, and luring you in with tastes or power or knowledge of the unknown. Many people do not believe possessions are real, but I know they can easily manipulate humans, animals, and inanimate objects, so to completely overtake a person is not out of the realm of possibility.

Satan serves God's glory against his will. God holds him bound and restrained. He carries out only those things which have been divinely permitted to him. He obeys his Creator because he is compelled to yield him service wherever God impels him. In the book of Job, Satan must ask permission to test Job. Remember in chapter 1, we talked about God putting a Cherubim as the same status of power as Satan, to protect the Garden of Eden? So, from the first human created, Satan has been trying to stop people from following God; and he is still at it today! Satan and his army will stop at nothing to get people to stop following God; because they know that God has total power and will ultimately have victory!

It's estimated by many Bible scholars that approximately twenty five percent of the miracles Jesus performed were casting demons out of people. Satan and his demons are not confined to the Bottomless Pit now. This event will not happen until Jesus returns to us in His second coming. Until that event happens, Satan and his demons are still free to roam in the air seeking who they are going to try and devour next.

One scripture showing their fear and belief in God's authority over them is, James 2:19, You believe that God is one. You do well; the demons also believe, and shudder. Demons at times come together in masses called Legion. Mark 5:2-10 says, When Jesus arrived at the country of the Gerasenes, He encountered a possessed man on the outside of the city in a cemetery. And when Jesus had stepped out of the boat, immediately there met him out of the tombs a man with an unclean spirit. He lived among the tombs. And no one could bind him anymore, not even with a chain, for he had often been bound with shackles and chains, but he wrenched the chains apart, and he broke the shackles in pieces. No one had the strength to subdue him. Night and day among the tombs and on the mountains, he was always crying out and cutting himself with stones. And when he saw Jesus from afar, he ran and fell before him. And crying out with a loud voice, he said, "What have you to do with me, Jesus, Son of the Highest God? I adjure you by God, do not torment me." For he was saying to him, "Come out of the man, your unclean spirit!" And Jesus asked him, "What is your name?" He replied, "My name is Legion, for we are many." And he begged him earnestly not to send them out of the country.

Demon possession and demon activity is more commonly recognized in third world countries. Many debates whether demons can possess believer, and follower of God. The Bible is silent concerning this but has a lot to say about their possible influence on us and of our need to be aware of their desire to adversely affect us. Jesus repeatedly told demons to "come out" of people, and the Bible records that Jesus "cast out" demons, several times as well as did his disciples.

There are stories in which a demonized person functioned normally part of the time. Other stories tell of the person being struck, deaf, dumb or in a coma like state, or obviously in complete control by something other than their natural self. We are not to be afraid of demons, God has power over them.

Luke 8:27-39 (NIV), *And when He stepped out on the land, there met Him a certain man from the city who had demons for a long time. And he wore no clothes, nor did he live in a house but in the tombs. When he saw Jesus, he cried out, fell before Him, and with a loud voice said, "What have I to do with You, Jesus, Son of the Highest God? I beg You, do not torment me!" For He had commanded the unclean spirit to come out of the man. For it had often seized him, and he was kept under guard, bound with chains and shackles; and he broke the bonds and was driven by the demon into the wilderness. Jesus asked him, saying, "What is your name?" And he said, "Légion," because many demons had entered him. And they begged Him that He would not command them to go out into the abyss. Now a herd of many swine was feeding there on the mountain. So, they begged Him that*

He would permit them to enter them. And He permitted them. Then the demons went out of the man and entered the swine, and the herd ran violently down the steep place into the lake and drowned. When those who fed, them saw what had happened, they fled and told it in the city and in the country. Then they went out to see what had happened, and came to Jesus, and found the man from whom the demons had departed, sitting at the feet of Jesus, clothed and in his right mind. And they were afraid. They also who whole multitude of the surrounding region of the Gadarenes asked Him to depart from them, for they were seized with great fear. And He got into the boat and returned. Now the man from whom the demons had departed begged Him that he might be with Him. But Jesus sent him away, saying, "Return to your own house, and tell what great things God has done for you." And he went his way and proclaimed throughout the whole city what great things Jesus had done for him.

Here, a demon of suicide repeatedly tried to drown a boy, and throw him into a fire, to kill him, and was not easy to make leave.

Mark 9:17-29 (NIV), *Then one of the crowds answered and said, "Teacher, I brought You my son, who has a mute spirit. And wherever it seizes him, it throws him down; he foams at the mouth, gnashes his teeth, and becomes rigid. So, I spoke to Your disciples, that they should cast it out, but they could not." He answered him and said, "O faithless generation, how long shall I be with you? How long shall I bear with you? Bring him to Me." Then they brought him to Him. And when he saw Him, immediately the spirit convulsed him, and he fell on the ground and wallowed, foaming at the mouth. So, He asked his father, "How long has this been happening to him?" And he said, "From childhood. And often he has thrown him both into the fire and into the water to destroy him. But if You can do anything, have compassion on us and help us." Jesus said to him, "If you can believe, all things are possible to him who believes." Immediately the father of the child cried out and said with tears, "Lord, I believe; help my unbelief!" When Jesus saw that the people came running together, He rebuked the unclean spirit, saying to it, "Deaf and dumb spirit, I command you, come out of him and enter him no more!" Then the spirit cried out, convulsed him greatly, and came out of him. And he became as one dead, so that many said, "He is dead." But Jesus took him by the hand and lifted him up, and he arose. And when He had come into the house, His disciples asked Him privately, "Why could we not cast it out?" So, He said to them, "This kind can come out by nothing but prayer and fasting."*

Several belief systems like the traditional Korean, think demons inhabit the natural world; and are attached to, and become part of household objects, and are present everywhere in numbers too great to count.

Inuit believe there are guardian spirits everywhere and possess both aspects of evil and good. They associate spirits with the elements of the earth, sea and sky. Even a stone has a guardian spirit in their beliefs.

Ancient Babylonians, believed demons could influence every part of their lives. Controlling every part of their body and their emotions at times.

Whether you believe there is an evil roaming the earth or not, I hope you enjoy reading the following stories of when I believe I encountered them.

There is No Protection in Daylight

I had created a theater group for our church youth. They were thriving in this new adventure, and coming out of their shy shells, realizing their individual gifts regarding acting, playwriting, set design and the like.

This Wednesday had been peaceful and uneventful. The sun shone brightly through the dining room window where I worked to finish writing a new play, we would practice for the first time that evening. I was excited to see everyone's reaction to it.

As I stood up to get more paper, a loud very deep mixture of human and animal growls came at me from the right side of my face. Thankfully, it did not show itself, but I could feel the hot damp breath full of a mix of rotten meat and sulfur stench. I froze but did not engage or acknowledge the presence in any way. I am sure it delighted in the fear that ran through me, chilling my blood as I felt it drain from the top of my body to my feet.

At this same instant, it sounded like huge boulders were being smashed on the roof above. I ran out the front door grasping to the hope there was a rational explanation for the sound, a group of trees falling on my roof or something, anything. As I stepped into the bright sunlight, the air was fresh and to my utter astonishment, nothing was amiss. There were birds in the feeder eating, and a cat stretched out across the sidewalk taking a nap. I couldn't believe it. The sound of falling boulders was deafening! Yet, obviously, it was not disturbing anything outside.

I went back inside, and there was a stillness, a heaviness in the air. Then it seemed to drop in temperature at a rapid rate. Once again, the sound of something very large and heavy being dropped on my roof began, along with a sort of trembling sound in the walls. I prayed out loud for God, and all the good angels to protect me from all evil and whatever had crossed my path to leave immediately in the name of God. It stopped in an instant.

Some people might find my feelings regarding my next tale odd coming from a Christian. On this occasion, an uninvited interaction with a self-proclaimed demon and myself, was an enlightening tool. It has changed how I judge the truth of what my clients tell me. Many times, the events relayed by someone involving the unseen realm, light or dark, are hard to take as complete truth, and not an over exaggeration by a frightened or possibly disturbed individual.

Look Again

It was a very cold deep winter day, I was in the back part of my front house that looks out over the acreage, and the fruit trees planted there. I had not been thinking about, or watching anything scary, dark, or paranormal.

I was looking at the snow drifting peacefully over the land and as beautiful as it was, I hoped my fruit trees would survive the extended freeze we were in. All the sudden, I felt a heaviness to the room and a silence fell over everything. I could no longer hear the usual house noises of clocks ticking, street traffic passing by, nothing. Then, in my mind, a deep seductive male voice said, "You only believe in what you can prove these days."

The voice sent a chill through me when it ended in a sort of raspy hiss. I knew it was a dark energy. From that realization, before I could pray to God to protect me, I seemed to go into a sort of trance, frozen like my trees.

The voice seemed amused. It said, "Humans are so easy to manipulate, you think you rule this world, but you don't. And you can't control what's happening to you now. Don't worry," he exhaled deeply, "I just want to visit, to correct your thinking."

Whatever this entity was, unfortunately it was in control, and all I could do was listen. This was not something that happens to me. I stay very guarded most of the time.

He went on to say, "You don't believe people when they tell you a demon came a calling!" he laughed. "Well I *am* one. I want you to remember this visit, so I'm going to let you." He continued in a deep throaty voice that was terrifying yet, inviting all at the same time. "Look outside again, what do you see, tell me?"

I felt like I had snapped out of the trance, and looking outside, I thought what just happened must have been an awful daydream or something. I didn't even care, my thoughts were only on the beautiful sunny day outside and where I could get enough containers to haul all the ripe pears in. I felt such an urgency to get the crops in before they rotted. The trees were so heavy with fruit, that the ground was blanketed with them!

It was the best crop I had ever had, and I was so excited, imagining all the preserves and desserts I would make. Then right before I turned to go search for baskets or containers, I felt a light touch run down my face and neck. Then a voice said, "Look again. Do you see how we can make you see things that aren't there, to feel things, and manipulate you with such ease?"

Looking back toward the window, I was more chilled that the temperature outside. My mind was racing trying to make sense of what just happened. The trees were like I originally saw them. Everything was frozen and lifeless. The only thing blanketing the ground was snow!

7

PRAYERS AND
PROTECTIONS

*H*umans have sought protection, blessings, and power for every area of their lives for many thousands of years. This practice runs through every spiritual practice and belief system. every race, the world over. Some of the most intense use of symbolism and amulets occurred in Asia, Rome, Greece, and Egypt, however, all tribes, and peoples have their fair share.

There is an instinctual desire to be safe from harm. Our DNA is hardwired with the instinct of survival, the same way animals, and all other species of living creatures are. It has been proven plants communicate when danger is upon them, they seek assistance.

When humans are faced with danger or stress, a biological trigger goes off, and an internal warning system kicks in. This could be connected to genetic memory, like the instinct that runs through all of us, and is part of a collective knowledge we all tap into. Perhaps this could explain how we have a familiarity to, and readily embrace and mimic the behaviors of our ancestors. We seek out our roots, our past, and perhaps this influences our belief system too. If throughout time, wearing, or carrying a certain item with a person saved them from danger, it becomes likely we would want that same perceived help, then would assign that item with the attribute to protect from a specific harm.

A common term for an object carried for protection is an amulet. Amulets symbolize strength and protection. They would be inscribed and painted specific colors associated with their belief system. They can be made of any material. Depending on the desired protection. Some prefer wood, others think gemstones, or other natural substances work best.

Another way to gain power or protection, is to call upon a powerful entity, or deity against attacks. Depending on the belief system in place, throughout history people have asked assistance from the upper and lower worlds, from God, or gods, and a multitude of angels and demons.

For example, let's look at two of the more than thirty-nine well known mythologies that have a fertility deity, god or goddess associated with them, to assist in pregnancy, childbirth, and protection of infants, who were so vulnerable to death throughout the ages. They are found in African mythology, and in the mythology of the Ancient Egyptians, Aztecs, Chinese, Celtic, Catholic hagiology (which is the writings and teachings dealing with the lives and legends of saints), Germanic, Greeks, Hawaiian, Hindus, Australian, Japanese, Native Americans, the Norse, Roman, and Haitian Voodoo mythology, just to name a few.

In Assyrian and Babylonian mythology, Pazuzu, who's height of worship seems to be late eighth century B.C. through the sixth century B.C., was the king of the demons of the wind, storms and drought. His brother was Humbaba, and his father was the god Hanbi.

Assyrian and Babylonian women would have petitioned the powerful ancient demon, Pazuzu, to help them not with matters of the elements around them, but to safely carry their child to a healthy natural birth and to be a powerful defense against demonic attacks from Lamashtu, a female demon with destructive powers, feared by pregnant women and those with newborns, who were her favorite victims.

Many of you who read about or saw the movie series of "The

Exorcist," which is about the possession of a young boy who played with a Ouija board, portrayed by a little girl, will find the name Pazuzu familiar as the possessing demon that one of the priests has come in contact with while participating in an archaeological dig.

While a Catholic believer today might ask either Saint Catherine, noted for her work as a nurse, mediator and spiritual leader during the 14th century, or Saint Anne of David's house and line, believed by some, to be the mother of the Virgin Mary, and grandmother of Jesus Christ, according to apocryphal Christian and Islamic tradition for assistance and protection.

There is a vast list of deities, charms, amulets and the like for every single malady, or desire you can think of. You can now as you always could, ask and receive, those favors from light entities or the dark entities, depending on your belief system. Both bringing about the desired result in many cases.

I want to cover something I feel many do without realizing it, when they go to sleep, and that is astral projection or travel, as it is commonly termed. Several clients of mine have told me the experience helped them realize that we are not our bodies, and that our consciousness lives on after death. By leaving the physical body they had previously considered to be the total representation of themselves, going into an unseen, alternate reality, then to return to the physical state once more, was a very moving, learning curve for them.

Many of you may have seen the movie, "Insidious." I thought it did a good job of portraying the possible low-level entities that linger around at times.

Is there any biblical reference to astral projection? I believe that is what the apostle Paul is talking about in 2 Corinthians 12:1–6 (NIV). Paul says, *"It is doubtless not profitable for me to boast. I will come to visions and revelations of the Lord: I know a man in Christ who fourteen years ago—whether in the body I do not know, or whether out of the body I do not know, God knows—such a one was caught up to the third heaven. And I know such a man—whether in the body or out of the body I do not know, God knows— how he was caught up into Paradise and heard inexpressible words, which it is not lawful for a man to utter. Of such a one I will boast; yet of myself I will not boast, except in my infirmities. For though I might desire to boast, I will not be a fool; for I will speak the truth. But I refrain, lest anyone should think of me above what he sees me to be or hears from me"*

There are scholars that feel Paul is talking about himself in third person as the man "caught up to the third heaven," in verse 7 he continues to relay his memories, "And lest I should be exalted above measure by the abundance of the revelations, a thorn in the flesh was given to me, a messenger of Satan to buffet me, lest I be exalted. The way he relays his thoughts to us, I believe the apostle Paul is referring to his own experience 14 years earlier.

I knew some of the dreams I remembered were vivid and felt so real, as well as the interactions I had during those travels. I never thought much about it, until the energy of an entity I had never encountered seemed to walk through my house one evening. It was that changing of the guard time of day when Night glides in tossing a big blanket of stars for her backdrop, on top of the last golden red ray following Day to their next dawn.

One of the most powerful and called upon Archangels is Saint Michael. This prayer is often used by people before and after they go on paranormal investigations, but of course can be used for your request of protection at any time or situation.

Opening Prayer

Saint Michael the Archangel defend us in battle,
Be our protection against the wickedness and snares of the Devil,
May God rebuke him, we humbly pray,
And do thou, O Prince of the heavenly host,
By the power of God, thrust into hell Satan and all evil spirits
Who wander through the world for the ruin of souls?
Amen

Closing prayer

In the name of Jesus Christ, I command all human spirits to be bound to the confines of the cemetery.
I command all inhuman spirits to go where Jesus Christ tells you to go, for it is He who commands you.
Amen

A favorite prayer of my mother was the 23rd Psalm. I said it at her bedside, as I was giving her last rights:

23rd Psalm

The Lord is my shepherd I shall not want.
He maketh me to lie down in green pastures
He leadeth me beside the still waters
He restoreth my soul
He leadeth me in the paths of righteousness for his name's sake
Yea, though I walk through the valley of the shadow of death,
I will fear no evil: for thou art with me; thy rod and thy staff they comfort me.
Thou preparest a table before me in the presence of mine enemies; thou annointest my head with oil; my cup runneth over
Surely goodness and mercy shall follow me all the days of my life.
and I will dwell in the house of The Lord forever.
Amen

St. Christopher Prayer for Travelers

Lord, we humbly ask you to give your Almighty protection to all travelers.
Accept our fervent and sincere prayers that through your great power and unfaltering spirit, those who travel may reach their destination safe and sound.

Grant your divine guidance and infinite wisdom to all who operate automobiles, trains, planes and boats. Inspire them with due sense of duty and knowledge and help them guide those entrusted in their care to complete their travel safely.

We thank you, Oh Lord, for your great mercy and unending love to all mankind and for extending your arm of protection to all travelers. Amen.

Prayers for Pets

Pet prayers and devotions help us pray for and offer gratitude for our dogs, cats, and other pets and farm and wild animals. In the Catholic and general tradition, animals are important: they are mentioned regularly in the Bible and throughout the writings of saints and theologians

Prayer for a sick animal
by Teal L. Gray

Heavenly Father,
you created all things for your glory
and made us stewards of this creature.
If it is your will, restore it to health and strength.
Blessed are you, Lord God,
and holy is your name for ever and ever.
Amen

Blessing For Animals

by Teal L. Gray

Blessed are you, Lord God,
maker of all living creatures,
On the fifth and sixth days of creation,

you called forth fish in the sea,
birds in the air and animals on the land.
You inspired St. Francis to call all animals
his brothers and sisters.
We ask you to bless this animal.
By the power of your love,
enable it to live per your plan.
May we always praise you
for all your beauty in creation.
Blessed are you, Lord our God, in all your creatures!
Amen

Protection during astral travel
by Athena C.

I learned two things very early on that I use every time I journey or do any sort of energy work. Whether your astral travel, spiritual journey, past life regression, self-hypnosis, remote viewing, energy healing, and so on, the first thing you need is a protected space.

Some people create this by placing certain stones around the room such as onyx, selenite and other stones used for grounding and protection. For me, I picture a bright white light (in my mind) that encompasses the room I am in. Then past that, I envision a gold light that is even farther out, and which protects me from any negative energies intruding into my space. Think about it like preventing a hacker from getting into your computer system. You can't see your computer system, but you know the safety program works.

The second thing is a way to get back to your physical self quickly without question. I relate it to swimming out in the ocean. The first time and I did not realize how far out I was and had a moment of fear about being able to get back to shore. With energy work, I picture a thick gold rope tied around my waist and anchored to the location of my physical body. This way, when I'm done with my journey or question, if I have traveled out of my comfort zone, I picture myself grabbing the golden rope and returning to my physical body with a feeling of safety and completion.

Think of Dorothy's red slippers in the movie "Wizard of OZ." Click your heels three times and you are home.

After journeying or taking in a new experience, always take a moment to ground yourself and rebalance your mind and energy, putting yourself back into the present and feeling a sense of calm. If you feel a little "out of it", that's normal. You might feel this when you are doing energy work, learning something new or having energy work done on you as a healing treatment such as Heal Touch or Reiki etc. I always have a glass of water handy to stay hydrated. This helps with the body's energy levels and brain function. The action of holding the glass and drinking helps bring me back to the present moment.

Protection Phrase
by Athena C.

So many people take classes on energy work, tarot card reading and many other things. Unfortunately, they are not also taught how to protect themselves from "bad" energy (spirits.) It's like being around somebody who is sick, and you catch their cold. So, if we are aware of it, we can take steps to protect ourselves.

When I was, young and would go to bed for the night, I always felt as if there were spirits of people who had passed wanting to talk to me. I was fearful because I didn't know what to do or say. Honestly, I was afraid and thought "what if they are not nice spirits?" Because reality is, not all spirits are good! My Mom told me to use the phrase, «What in God's name do you want?» She said if they are bad spirits, they will go away when you ask them that. Think about it like dowsing a vampire with holy water like they do in the movies. I still use that phrase to this day. My belief is that I am calling on a higher power of light (of good.) Be it God, Archangel Michael, Allah, Hashem, Vishnu, Mother Earth. You can insert any word or make up any phrase that calls on a higher power in the metaphysical world than yourself. I think of it as having a bodyguard for protection.

STORIES AND
VALADATIONS

$\mathcal{I}$ met Teal at a conference a few years ago. I have never met a more genuine person. She is sweet, kind, considerate, and above all honest.

Teal and I hit it off right away. We laughed and joked with one another like we had been friends for years so when I had something happening to me, Teal was the first person I thought to call. My husband and I had just moved to some new property with a new home built and all of our belongings still packed up in the new shop next to our home. My mother had passed away years ago and I had her precious collection of music boxes stored in the shop. They had been wrapped in bubble wrap and carefully packed, by me. These music boxes are not the battery-operated kind but, the wind-up type. The story that follows is completely true and I have peace about it thanks to Teal.

My husband and I were staying in an RV parked in front of the house being completed. He was out tractoring around the property and I went to the shop to get something I needed. When I opened the door, I heard music. I stopped and listened and realized one of mom's music boxes was playing. The box that held these music boxes was way in the back and under a couple more moving boxes so I couldn't get to the exact box. The music kept playing and I thought, "Hi Mom, I miss you too." When my husband came in later that day, I told him about this and he said "yeah, it's been playing a couple of days."

These boxes don't play that long, you know the type, wind, listen, wind, listen... Anyway, we both had a laugh about it and thought mom was just making her presence known. Then the next morning I got up with a song stuck in my head that is a song I relate to my late brother. He passed away a few years ago. I couldn't get that song out of my head for another whole day and finally I decided mom and Rollie were trying to tell me something.

I called Teal and asked if she could do a tarot reading for me and she said "of course, after work today." Well we had set it up to meet on Facebook at six that evening, and Teal would do the reading over the internet. (Yes, she is that good at it!)

When we got together, Teal told me to think of the question I needed answered, so both Dave, my husband, and I sat there thinking about it. The next few things Teal said/asked me blew both Dave and I away. Teal had hit my very question head on without the cards. She answered everything and more in less than an hour. When we were finished, I was in tears and Dave was in AWE!

Teal told me things that neither Dave nor I have ever told her or anyone she may know. She hit on things more than thirty years old and gave us both peace of mind before we were finished. I can't stress enough how much this lady means to me. Not only is she gifted but, she is not in it for money. Teal never charged me one dime.

T. Jones

* * *

The evening that I meet Teal was at a paranormal investigation that we were both at. While others were investigating some of us were gathered in the living room of the house. Teal was there and began to give informal readings to all that were there. I cannot begin to express how at awe I was at how gifted she is. She got around to me, I was excited and nervous at the same time. She picked up right away on the fact that I was exploring the religion of practicing Voodoo. She advised me to steer away from that and follow more of a natural Magic practice. She informed me that I was a natural, that I possess natural / real Magic. I am still trying to figure that one out but have finally picked a path that feels right in that realm. As our reading progressed, she let me know that I have lived many past lives and might even have been an Egyptian High Priestess. Then all of the sudden she got very quiet and informed me that My Angel had just manifested in front of me, kind of acting like a shield. She began to explain to all in the room about true Guardian Angels and that I was one of the fortunate to have one. She began to describe my angle and said that she now understands why my path might be the way it is. She described angel as half white and half Black. She has One white wing and one Black wing, the arm on the black wing side has black flowing filigree coming down it. She also has a little black on her side, some on her face and hair as well. I cannot tell you how utterly speechless I was at the time. I just wanted to know more about her but did not want to interfere with others that were waiting for their turn bot be read. I have been talking to my angle more since my amazing reading with Teal and look forward to being able to see her for myself one day.

*   *   *

When I sat down with Teal, the first time, I had hopes of my mom coming through to say something, really anything, because I missed her more than I ever thought was possible. She had died four years prior to this and about 6 months after my divorce. Teal starts reading the cards and suddenly tells me that she sees me having lots of fun, dating different men and then she giggles. She went on to tell me that this was all fun and well but that within the next six months I would be faced with a hard decision because my true soul mate, love of my life, would possibly be looked over in my dating. "What? No, wait. That's not fair!" I said. She went on to say that I would be with one man who seemed like the perfect man for me and I would possibly miss my soul mate. The only way I would not miss him would be to be stay open to dating and not settle on the one I thought was right because he wasn't. Wow, the pressure, the uncertainty, this was all more than I expected, and I was fine being alone, but this was intriguing and scary all rolled into one crazy thought. She continued to describe a man that would be just what I had been hoping for and not at all my usual type, once again verifying that I would probably overlook him. After that bit of news, she did go on to tell me that my mom is with me all the time and that she was actually disappointed that I wasn't writing anymore. How in the world did Teal know that I had written for magazines before I moved to Texas and that I had several half-done manuscripts laying around? My mom told her, and my mom was right that I had not been writing, at all. We spoke of different lovely things about my mom and how much I missed her, but I could not get this perfect man getting away from me idea out of my head. Eventually it passed and I figured I had missed him, or she was wrong.

Exactly, six months, to the day, yes to the day, I went on a date with a man I had met, and he was not my usual type at all. I had been dating someone else that I thought was great and he was exactly the type I usually like, but it was just not feeling good. The unexpectedly wonderful date turned out to be a three-hour conversation with laughing, swapping stories of our childhood that were so similar and a several hour phone conversation that night. I honestly did not even think of Teal during all of this until a few weeks later when my new found love was the only man I cared to talk to or spend time with and I realized I had my first date with him on the exact day, six months after my meeting with Teal.

He got to meet Teal six months after our first date and she lit up when she saw him. She mentioned that she greatly enjoyed seeing him in real life, with me, after seeing him in the past, before I had met him. She was genuinely happy and so am I. We are still together, 16 months so far, and he is truly the love of my life, my soul mate and my total opposite! My writing is getting started again and I feel that is in part to the new happiness I have found that has allowed me to be me which is exactly what my mom would want.

Teal has continued to check in here and there. She does not just tell you something and move on. She feels it and desires to help you achieve the things she sees for you. Thank you, Teal, for helping me to keep my eyes open and my heart, especially.

*   *   *

I own a company called Dearly Departed Tours in Hollywood. We deal with a rather macabre subject of celebrity death in a light-hearted, respectful way.

I had the good fortune of spending a bit of time with Teal Gray when I visited Texas for the Dash Beardsley event. For the event I brought along some of the notorious artifacts from my bizarre collection. I brought a piece of the Hindenburg, a stone from the Sharon Tate fireplace, a piece of Carole Lombard's plane crash, a post from Rock Hudson's death bed... Teal expressed interest in seeing them.

The readings she got from the artifacts were so interesting. She recommended my not explaining each item, but to let her experience them for herself. It was uncanny and quite emotional to see her react to the different people and events. The thoughts that were provoked by the objects were spot on, and in some cases, comforting. These souls are not forgotten which is the most important thing.

Teal isn't someone who was selfish with her gifts, rather she is kind and generous. In my opinion she is ultimately concerned with the general GOOD of the world and of people. She spent hours of her time with myself and my husband Troy, giving us her interpretations, we can use to better ourselves and our career. Teal also brought forth a message from my recently deceased mother. A message that meant the world to me. You know how the gays are about their mothers.

Teal alerted us to a potentially malicious spirit in our storefront in Hollywood and gave us instructions about how to deal with her. Now that we know of this spirit's existence, we're able to appease her and "maintain" her. It's not an ideal situation, but it's good to know why things get so haywire occasionally.

I haven't spent much time with Teal in person, but I feel a deep connection. I think it's because I'm drawn to a person who is good.

Impressions of Objects I held in a Blind Test- Teal Gray

Tate Stone- I was immediately given the feeling of being jolted from a feeling of safety, love and security, with the image of pretty wallpaper and a female hand gliding over it to turn on a light in a room. I felt bedroom but could have been a sitting room. It was their inner sanctum so to speak, their haven. Then straight to confusion and sheer panic and fear. Pleading and I physically held my stomach. I kept smelling a strong smell of coffee but never saw cups or a pot, just a strong coffee smell and violent slashing, gunshots and blood. I felt like I was negotiating for a life. It was something I have never felt on that level, "Take me, spare him" impression. All the while images of slashing skin, choking on blood and everything being so loud added to the confusion of the moments. I was given the knowledge that although this Spirit's live had been stolen, they were at peace. They were not earth bound but had and did visit.

John Denver's plane- I felt so free holding this piece of medal. I felt alive in a way where all my senses were firing. Sheer joy. I saw lovely blue and light. Then somethings wrong, I'm feeling panic and I'm getting the impression of trying everything to fix whatever has happened. I can't, so I make peace with it, I know death is coming. I have tears run down my cheeks and all I see is darkness. A hard impact and it just goes black.

Rock's Bed- I felt the image of a beautiful room, but the piece I was holding had its own identity, it was important and had many stories to tell. I felt it had actual caring for the person that laid upon it, it's a bed. There is a flash of many lovers, beautiful hopeful trysts. But I feel empty, I feel I never can find peace. I am taken to the end that is with this piece, so the person it cared for deeply has died with it, on it. The end was a flash of so many beautiful memories mixed with longing. The memories become like real life and I feel like I go in and out of reality to the past. I feel desperate to stay, but then release.

The Hindenburg- This piece immediately overpowered me with souls desperate to tell their stories. So many all at once. So much unfinished business, "we were almost there," they say. I am almost unable to speak; I am crying, and I can't stop shaking and they are all trying to speak through me at once. I see excitement and a feeling of importance, privilege, then fear and disbelief, everything's on fire! It happens in an instant. We are flying then we're on fire, burning alive while others live. I did not shake the overwhelming experience of holding this piece for several days.

Blessings, Teal Gray

*   *   *

I had the pleasure of meeting Teal at a paranormal conference in Gainesville, TX. When she walked in the room, I didn't know who she was, but then she started talking to me and reading me. She told me that I was a healer (I work in the medical field in physical therapy) and that I was very grounded in nature (I am). She told me more about myself and my past that was just unbelievable to me. She even went some into my ancestry and was 100% correct with her reading, I was so floored with what she told me that I got extremely emotional. She validated some things I had been questioning which made a huge difference in my life. I had never believed in psychic mediums before then, but now I completely believe in Teal! She really helped me let go of some baggage I had been carrying and helped me change my path in life to a more positive direction. I will always be thankful to God for the interaction I had with Teal.

*   *   *

I have been through a lot of bumps in life but last year was one of the most difficult times in my life. Not knowing what to do or who to talk to, God put an Angel in my life. Since then I realized that things happened for a reason. I met Teal Gray at a psychic fair and had my reading and like all the other times with any other reading I didn't pay attention to what she told me until everything she had told me was been crystalized. At that moment I knew I had to go back and see her again and full of anxiety, fear, tears and confusion, she and her spirits guided me. Again, I was not sure whether to believe her or not but as time went by, I realized that again everything was coming true. Now I can confirm that Teal Gray is accurate and will give you the best advice but it's up to you if you want to take it. She is awesome and will always tell you the truth even if it hurts but sometimes it's better to be honest than for a person to lie to you. Since then I know I can trust her and recommend her to anyone looking for an honest psychic.

* * *

Hello Teal & happy New Year! I am reaching out to you to share how the reading has truly inspired me and helped me continue thriving as a journalist. I'd also love to have a session with you again in the future and I have definitely not forgotten about you! Have a wonderful day.

* * *

Thank you so much for the opportunity to write about Teal Gray! She is the most noted psychic I know and a very good friend. She is honest and true with regard to everything especially her gifts. She has given me the best readings of my life...which brought about change and the love of my life. I know you will do well in reading her upcoming book "Reading the Unwritten."

* * *

Teal, I met you at the Dallas Psychic fair in September. I am the inspiring book writer that gave you goose bumps knowing my calling was to write a book and I have started. I asked about my boys and you gave great insight. But most importantly you talked about my mom you gave me very profound news that normally you do not discuss. But you were straight and told be the number 8 to 10 not knowing if it was days, weeks or months but you told me to get my affairs with her in order. 6 weeks later I booked a trip to Boston then drove into NH to surprise my mother for her 70th Birthday. My sister came from Conn. and three other siblings came. We took her out on her Birthday just the children she brought into this world. It was just the six of us and the evening was amazing for all of us. I just wanted to say Thank you-Because you did this. If it was not for you telling me what I needed to know the trip would have never happened. And we would have missed the opportunity to all be together before she passed away. Thank you again.

* * *

Thank you for the amazing reading. I appreciate all your help and advice. You gave me that little push to keep on going.

* * *

Teal Gray has read for me many times, and I am always amazed at her abilities. She helps you understand your own path, and what your past loved ones and guides are trying to tell you. She is truly a blessing.

-SH

* * *

I have read all of Teal's books! and I am always impressed with her depth of knowledge and ability to write in a way that is understandable to the average reader. That makes her information important and her books of more interest to a wider audience they are well worth the read.

* * *

Being the Owner of Haunted Hill House
I have encountered several types of entities
Both Negative and Positive I have watched as Teal
Has seen and communicated with them as well
Teal Gray is my go to person
She is very enlightened
My visions and dreams have confusion sometimes
And Teal has a Unique Understanding to Interpret the meanings
Teal Gray is truly blessed and can see beyond the veil
Kathy Estes
Haunted Hill House

* * *

I'm honored to know Teal Gray, she is one of the most interesting and informative authors I have ever read. Her style of writing grabs your attention and you can't stop until you've finished her book. It is obvious that Teal does her research. She also is gifted with the ability to know, see and read things the average person can't. She did the most accurate tea leaf reading for me I was astonished at the information she gave me.

S.G

* * *

Teal Gray's ability to communicate with the "other side" is amazing! The amount of detail she is able to receive and communicate is astonishing. I have witnessed Teal's gift first hand. Her communication and compassion when receiving messages will make you a believer in miracles. She is the real deal.

Love ya Teal :)
Becky :)

* * *

Teal Gray is the real deal hands down, I have witnessed first hand her abilities to communicate with the other side. We have been on investigations where I only know the history and she is spot on who we know she is communicating with. The way she can help and heal others with her abilities in receiving messages is beyond amazing! Teal is the real deal!

*   *   *

I had a Tarot reading from Teal at an event shortly after I first met her. Before I could ask the specific questions that I had written down for her, Teal went off on a surprising tangent. For some reason, she zeroed in on a family member of mine who was going through a difficult time. Teal warned that this person was putting on a brave front, and that they were actually suicidal.

As you can imagine, I was quite shaken up by this. And, yes, I was even skeptical because I had recently spoken to this person and they had assured me they were fine. Even so, I immediately called my relative. At first, they repeated that they were OK. But when I told them about my reading with Teal and shared some notes from my reading, they finally admitted the truth. They were having suicidal thoughts!

This person now sees a therapist and is doing much, much better. I shudder to think what might have happened if Teal had not jumped in with this information. I had not even planned to ask about that situation. Teal's reading truly helped me and my family member achieve a deeper relationship.

Since that first reading with Teal, I have attended many events where Teal gave readings. Since I'm also an author, I often have the booth beside hers. Even so, I barely get a chance to talk to her at these events because Teal's reputation is such that she is booked solid. People drive long distances and patiently wait their turn. Teal does her best to make time for every single one of them. I often have seen Teal's friends and family pack up her entire booth while she continues giving readings. The whole room will be empty except for Teal and her client, the two of them completely caught up in their conversation.

One time, after a particularly busy event, Teal and I returned to the BNB we were sharing. After giving readings all day, several people, including me, saw bright green orbs flitting around Teal! It reminded me of static electricity, except it was yellow-green sparks!

- Tui Snider

* * *

My experiences with Teal have been nothing short of amazing. She is a shining light and a blessing in this world. She was able to help me identify some of my unhealed trauma from childhood and get closure on a situation with a loved one on the other side. She was able to connect me with loved ones on the other side and give messages that were detailed and no one else could have known. She has helped bring understanding and peace into my life.

She predicted that I would get pregnant when I thought I could not, Now I've got a beautiful, healthy 1 year old daughter Sidney! Thank you, Thank you, Thank you Teal! Stephanie M

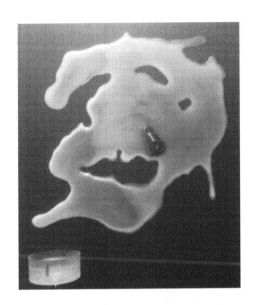

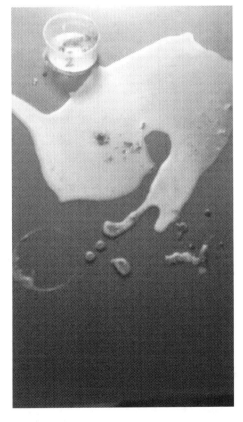

THELAVENDERCROW

ABOUT THE AUTHOR

Teal Gray Rev., N.D. Intuitive Empath,
Tea Leaf and Tarot Reader

*T*eal is a natural born Empath and Clairvoyant. For over 25 years she has used her gifts to help others find clarity in their lives. She uses Tea Leaf Readings and Tarot along with her natural gifts and abilities to unveil the mysteries that are within you and to empower your relationships and navigate through life's challenges. She generally asks you on what area of your life you would like to focus. The reading flows and information springs to life from there! Teal shares what she sees, good or bad. She believes that with Spiritual Guidance you can gain the power to make your dreams a reality and realize your higher spiritual self.

Writer, sacred site traveler, radio host of Para Mysteries and founder of Teal Gray Worldwide Investigative Team. She has used her gift of intuition and mediumship to help many paranormal investigative teams on sites of everything from historic buildings, homes around the world, and sacred sites. Through these many experiences she has amassed a greater understanding of the unknown. Sharing that knowledge is her passion.

Teal is a long-time student of Astrology and Member of the American Federation of Astrologers. Currently she is working on her Advanced Masters Diploma with Specialization through Kepler

College. Check out her column "Horoscopes and Insights" in the Dallas Entertainment Journal: http://dallasentertainmentjournal.com/category/horoscopes-and-insights-by-teal-gray/

She received her Doctorate in Holistic Health from American Institute of Holistic Theology. Ordained in New Your October 2011 as a Non-Denominational/Interfaith Minister through American Institute of Holistic Theology and Order of Universal Interfaith (OUNl). She is also a member of A World Alliance of Interfaith Clergy (AWAIC).

"Reading the Unwritten" is her fourth book.
She is the best-selling author of *Shades of Angels, Spirited Tales, and Scared Senseless.*

A native Texan, she is a city girl living her country girl dream with her home grown, harvested, arts and craft, nature crafts products company The Lavender Crow. Where products are infused with holy water and sacred oils from her sacred site travels.

Graduate of American Institute of Holistic Theology Doctor of Naturology, N.D. and Theological Studies leading to Ordainment as a Non-Denominational Interfaith Minister 201. Certificate of Ordination OUnI The Order of Universal Interfaith 2011

- Owner of The Lavender Crow, Purifying Products, Nature Crafts and Cool Stitches
- Certified Holistic Health Practitioner
- Member of American Association of Drugless Practitioners
- Certified Essential Oil Coach
- Ongoing Certification in Counseling and Eco-Art Therapy

Printed in the United States
By Bookmasters